# THE BOOK OF PANTO

# THE BOOK OF PANTO

CRAIG REVEL HORWOOD

faber

First published in 2026
by Faber & Faber Limited
The Bindery, 51 Hatton Garden
London EC1N 8HN

Typeset by Faber & Faber Limited
Printed and bound in the UK by CPI Group (UK) Ltd, Croydon, CR0 4YY



A CIP record for this book
is available from the British Library

ISBN 978–0–571–39367–1

MIX
Paper | Supporting responsible forestry
FSC® C013604

Printed and bound in the UK on FSC® certified paper in line with our continuing commitment to ethical business practices, sustainability and the environment.
**For further information see faber.co.uk/environmental-policy**

Our authorised representative in the EU for product safety is
Easy Access System Europe, Mustamäe tee 50, 10621 Tallinn, Estonia
gpsr.requests@easproject.com

2 4 6 8 10 9 7 5 3 1

For my wonderful Mum,

**Beverley Horwood OAM**

From the very beginning, you believed in me, encouraged my dreams, and somehow managed to support every outrageous costume.

This book (and so much of my life) would never have been possible without you.

# CONTENTS

# INTRODUCTION

Panto is in the blood in Britain. I mean, you only have to say, 'Oh no, it isn't!' and everyone around you will shout, 'Oh yes, it is!' in reply. In Australia, where I grew up and studied musical theatre, we don't really have a big culture of going to pantomime, so it wasn't overly familiar to me as a kid.

When I look back, however, we did have our own version of it as a family, when we used to put Christmas shows on. We didn't have mobile phones or the internet, and TV was limited to a small number of channels – not like cable or the endless choices you have on streaming today; the only reliable entertainment you had at Christmas back then was what you created for yourselves. We'd write our own scripts, we'd sing songs, we'd do old skits and pretend to be ghosts and ghouls, diving into our dress-up box for costumes. It was so much fun for us and became something we did every year after Christmas dinner. I guess it kept us children occupied and out of the adults' hair, but it also really gave us performance and communication skills.

That Christmas show had elements of pantomime – the festive occasion, the dressing up and gathering round with family – but it wasn't *quite* the same, of course. I wish we had pantomime as a tradition in Australia. Apart from being huge fun, it's a really good introduction to live theatre and it gets you over that hurdle of being afraid to go out and sit with a bunch of people you don't know. When you're in the theatre, enjoying the same form of entertainment, laughing at the same jokes, it automatically makes you part of a community.

I would be lying if I said that I fell in love with pantomime straight away. I did act in one in Australia, when I was twenty – it was *Jack and the Beanstalk* at a small but popular venue in Sydney, called Phillip Street Theatre. Even then, in my first panto, I was playing the villain: Freddy Fleshcreep. I remember singing contemporary pop songs, like Michael Jackson's 'Bad', but that's about it. I certainly don't recall understanding pantomime as a genre. I thought it was just for kids; I'd never considered it a legitimate type of art. There was a general attitude towards actors in pantomime of: 'Oh God, they're in panto, that's the end of their career.' Possibly as a result of that, I had no respect for it, so I never thought that I would ever get involved again myself.

I moved to the UK in my twenties, where I worked as a dancer until the age of thirty and performed in musicals, then became an associate director and then a director-choreographer, gradually stopping performing. That is, until producers Michael Harrison and Jonathan Kiley – who used to run the company Qdos Pantomime, which was bought by Crossroads Pantomime in 2021 – had the bright idea for me to play a villain in a panto after seeing me as a judge on *Strictly Come Dancing*. They tested me for a season. I thought I would be awful as by that point, I hadn't been on stage for sixteen years. Most people who perform in pantomime master the genre by working in the chorus to start with, then coming up through the ranks and learning from the principal players as they do so. By the time they have lead roles, they're used to the ad libs and the fluidity of pantomime. But I was walking in comparatively blind, with my one stint in *Jack and the Beanstalk* in Australia a good while in the past. Michael and Jonathan said, 'Just give it a try: we'd like you to play the Evil Queen in *Snow White and the Seven Dwarfs*.' I figured I'd give it a bash. It was a production at Venue Cymru in Llandudno, North Wales – a lovely big theatre, and a good testing ground for newbies to panto.

I was *so* overweight – I mean, I had a fifty-two-inch waist – so it was a massive shock having to get back into shape for being on stage. Michael and Jonathan booked me because I had become known for being the 'mean' judge on *Strictly*. They didn't know or care if I could sing, let alone act, so I think they were happily surprised when I came to rehearsals and could do both. As for the costumes, I'd only ever done drag at parties, and in *La Cage aux Folles* back in 1985, when I played one of Les Cagelles, the dancers who worked at the drag nightclub on the French Riviera where the musical is set. I learned a lot about make-up performing in *La Cage aux Folles* – it's such an incredible piece of theatre to be in – but it wasn't the same as pantomime make-up, so I had to learn quickly what panto drag required. What with that and all the corsets, eyelashes, wigs and numerous dress changes required for the role of the Evil Queen, I was thrown in at the deep end.

The first week of shows was terrible. I hated every minute of it. I didn't know what to expect and had to learn a lot, very quickly. As a dancer or when acting in musicals, you aren't trained to communicate with an audience – beyond projecting properly – and breaking the fourth wall, the imaginary barrier separating actors from from audience, was totally different from what I was used to. That, and I wasn't ready for so much ad libbing. I didn't realise at the time that the ad libs are generally *not* ad libs as such. They're usually prepared beforehand: you'll have a list written down to choose from on any given night. It means you never get really caught out without a funny line. But I wasn't armed with those when I started out. I was treating it too seriously as an actor, too, presenting myself as a polished musical theatre version of the Evil Queen rather than leaning into my *Strictly* 'villain' persona. I was used to getting into character and staying in it without doing those knowing winks to the audience that you have in panto.

The second week was just as bad. I hadn't worn heels for years and was still adjusting to being back on stage after such a long break. Sometimes there were three shows a day – on Sundays there would be one at ten in the morning, then an afternoon show and then an evening show. That after a performance on the Saturday night nearly did me in!

But by the third week, I'd lost two stone and was starting to get fitter. I had to have all my costumes taken in by six inches. When I did an interview with Michael Hogan in the *Guardian* back in 2019, he joked that I should patent the panto diet: eat whatever you feel like over Christmas and still lose weight, because you're burning it all off in the performances.

Unfortunately, I pushed myself a bit too hard and I got injured, because I was throwing myself into it wholeheartedly after not having danced for so long, so I had to go on painkillers and was having physio every single day. It was like getting a vintage car working again.

Little by little, though, I found myself enjoying pantomime. I still didn't fully understand it, but Jonathan Kiley was a brilliant teacher, showing me how I could play with the audience and deviate from the script. That freedom was incredible to me, though it took some time to get used to talking to the audience – never mind them booing and that being a good thing!

I started to appreciate what an art there is to pantomime, and how difficult it is. It's more difficult than doing a musical, I think – you're dancing, you're acting, but then there's a much more symbiotic relationship with the audience. And you'll often find yourself playing multiple parts in panto. In *Snow White*, I was playing the Evil Queen and the old lady, of course, who she turns into to make Snow White eat the poisoned apple, and then I was breaking character to be 'Craig Revel Horwood, judge off *Strictly Come Dancing*'. It took a while to get my head round it, but when I did, I found the whole thing immense fun.

Then I got a terrible review. I remember it was a double-page spread, with a headline mimicking me as I am on *Strictly Come Dancing*, something like 'Far from fab-u-lous'. They said I was an old fat queen in drag, and who needed to see that on stage. I thought that was my panto career over there and then, but thankfully Michael and Jonathan invited me back to appear the following year. People had apparently written to the newspaper, up in arms about the negative comments, and said the reviewer was wrong. That's the glorious thing about pantomime: more than any art form, the audience is a crucial part of it. And if the audience loves you, that's all that counts.

I played the Evil Queen in *Snow White* for three years, I think, and then they tried me as the Wicked Stepmother in *Cinderella*, then as Hook in *Peter Pan*. Pantomimes are a bit like musicals on acid: they require a mix of classical training, jazz training and musicals experience. That said, once you've learned the craft of panto, you do see similarities that crop up across the different productions that can help you find your feet quickly once you've done two or three. The jokes are usually variations on a theme, and generally delivered with the same verve and intention; it's just the characters that change. Even then, they're 'stock' roles: the hero, the heroine, the villain, the comic foil and so on. All the shows have plenty of double entendres, the smutty jokes that go over the children's heads. Then there are jokes specifically aimed at the kids, so everyone's laughing, but for different reasons. And the productions always have clever scripts. Yes, they're formulaic, but they're also topical and have to appeal to all ages and demographics.

That's what keeps pulling me back to pantomime. If you go to a Taylor Swift concert, you know the audience is going to be made up of Swifties, i.e. mostly girls of a certain age. Or when you go to see boy bands like Take That or Westlife, the crowd is likely going to be women around forty-five years old, who loved them thirty years ago. But when I look out from the stage of whatever pantomime show I'm in, every year without fail, the audience is full of people of all ages, ethnicities, sexualities . . . The kids don't have to turn around when they hear a joke and say, 'What do they mean by that? Why is it so funny?' because even the rude jokes are delivered with such physical humour (such as a very visible wink to the audience) that the kids can enjoy them, and the parents can chuckle to themselves, appreciating the joke on a different level. Panto is for everyone: no matter where you work and no matter what you do, whether you're a high court judge or a toilet cleaner, you're all having the same experience. It's deeply ingrained within the community, because it brings people together.

In some ways, pantomime reminds me of *Strictly Come Dancing*. Both have touched the hearts and minds of the nation and given them something to get excited by and people to root for and aspire to be like. They're good entertainment for three-year-olds *and* ninety-three-year-olds alike. And I'm the villain in both . . . In fact, *Strictly* has found its way into pantomimes across the country, with productions adding in a 'good judge' and an 'evil judge', who score the dancers in the show. I've had kids come up to me saying, 'I'm playing you in my pantomime at school!'

I do feel ashamed of how rude I was about pantomime when I was younger. How dare I even consider slagging it off, thinking it was a terrible, sub-art form?! So much hard work, expertise, care and craftsmanship go into it. The writers who do the scripts for panto productions each year have to do lots of research to ensure they know the surrounding areas of each venue, and the local politics, to be able to make the shows topical and fun for each particular audience. Those in-jokes make people in the audience feel even more a part of the community, because 'outsiders' won't get them in quite the same way.

When the Covid pandemic hit and all the theatres closed down, people really missed live entertainment. And of course it has an impact on us if we can't go to something we're accustomed to seeing every year with friends and relatives. Covid taught us all a valuable lesson: that we *do* need to be together. We need to experience things with other human beings – laughing together, booing together, being scared together, cheering together – and we were starved of that for a time. It had a profound effect on the industry, as well as audiences. I felt people had a newfound appreciation for panto when shows came back on; as performers, we could feel the audiences' excitement to be back in the theatre and that is reflected in the fact that post-pandemic pantomime ticket sales have broken records each year since.[1]

I live in a village of around fifteen hundred people and they all come out to watch the local panto, including me. Unusually, it's put on in March, which, given I'm performing in panto from November to January, makes it a rare one that I can actually make it along to. It runs for a week and everyone loves it. In many ways, it's just like the big pantomimes that get put on in cities – the stories are the same, the roles are the same, the costumes will look similar and you have the usual 'Oh no, he didn't!', 'Oh yes, he did!' audience interaction. But what's wonderful is that it is hyper-localised. We all know each other, and when people perform in the panto, we get to see a different side to them – the gardener's up there doing a dance, for instance. It becomes a celebration of everything the village has achieved in the year and a way for us all to gather together and have fun. You'll hear very different reactions to local performances like this compared to the big professional shows. As a small community, everyone in the audience has an investment in every single person on the stage: maybe that's because they're your vet or your GP, or maybe you've provided the dress for the person playing the Dame or a prop for Buttons, or maybe you're helping put on tea and cake in the interval. At its heart, that's what pantomime is about, and getting to watch it in my home area really has helped me appreciate it on a new level.

It's nearly twenty years since I started doing panto and I've only come to love it more over that time. Through the pages of this book, I look back at its evolution into the form we see on stage today, and talk to my fellow performers and professionals in the business about their experiences of and reflections on the wonderful world of pantomime. Plus, I'll tell you a few fun tales from my own time walking the boards as some of panto's most wicked – and wickedly fun – villains.

GUEST STAR

# SIR DAVID SUCHET

One of the many fun aspects of acting in pantomime is that you become part of a world of people who share your love for it. I wanted to talk to some performers for this book who, like me, had come into the genre from other backgrounds, to hear about their experiences and thoughts about this too often overlooked theatrical form. First up is the wonderful Sir David Suchet, beloved actor of many roles, most famously that of Agatha Christie's twirly mustachioed detective, Hercule Poirot. He made his pantomime debut as Captain Hook in *Peter Pan* at the Bristol Hippodrome in the 2023–4 season.

*We've both played Hook – such a fun role – and I wondered how you found playing a villain, and whether you'd have preferred to play one of the 'good' characters instead?*

Captain Hook was a joy to play. He is such an iconic character. I love playing villains! In fact, before my role as Hercule Poirot my career was dominated by my playing villainous roles both in the theatre and on screen. I was awarded an Emmy for playing Robert Maxwell!

*Did you go to pantomimes as a child and if so, what are your memories of it?*

I remember the first panto I was taken to. It made a huge impression on me. My grandmother took me to *Where the Rainbow Ends.* I now know that it is not considered a pantomime in the true sense of the word (it has no Dame), but it was my very first experience of seeing fairies and angels and suits of armour actually moving on a stage! After that we used to go to our local theatre and on a regular basis to the pantomimes at the Golders Green Hippodrome.

*Did you have preconceptions about pantomime before acting in it?*

Ever since I was a child, I have enjoyed going to see pantomimes, but I had no preconceptions about acting in them: I knew what was needed but didn't have any idea about what to expect.

*Pantomime is a genre that is heavily reliant on audience interaction. How do you find the dynamic with the audience, particularly with pantomime having such a range of ages coming to see it?*

This was the most challenging for me. I had never been on any stage – ever – and been booed one minute and cheered at the next! I'd also never been on stage and had children running about the auditorium with sparklers (battery operated) and talking loudly and sometimes yelling at me! I don't know if I ever got used to it, but I enjoyed it enormously.

*As someone who has performed in many Shakespeare productions with the RSC, did you find parallels between Shakespeare's plays and pantomime? This has come up when I'm speaking to frequent pantomime performers: they see panto as being very much in the tradition of Shakespeare's theatre work.*

Certainly. Shakespeare expected there to be audience participation with his 'Fools', and I know that Shakespeare's soliloquies are meant to be spoken directly to the audience. Apart from those examples I am not sure that I could make a general statement about pantomime being in the tradition of Shakespeare. It obviously originated from the Italian *commedia dell'arte* and as you've explored, in the eighteenth century, John Rich popularised the 'harlequinade' in London. And today much of our pantomime draws on the tradition of the music hall.

*Coming from a musicals background, I was amazed how much of a physical test pantomime turned out to be when I first did it. What did you find to be the hardest aspect of the genre as a newcomer to it?*

One word – endurance. The physical demands should never be exaggerated. I went into physical training long beforehand as I knew that this was going to be one of the most challenging aspects of me, at the age of seventy-seven, playing Captain Hook. I went home totally exhausted every single performance night. Remember, in pantomime there are two performances daily.

*You've performed in drag as Lady Bracknell – could you be lured back to the pantomime stage as an arch villainess?*

Everything in me would love to return to pantomime and I would only ever consider either the Dame (a traditional one, e.g. in *Mother Goose*) or the lead villain. I wouldn't want to play an arch villainess. Whether I could perform in pantomime now at the age of eighty, though, is very doubtful.

*My local village puts on a panto every year in March and I love to go along. Do you go to watch pantomimes now, and if so, do you have a favourite panto story and venue to see it in?*

I now go to pantomimes with my grandchildren and to see my theatre mates perform. I enjoy seeing those with whom I shared the stage at the Bristol Hippodrome. I will treasure the on-stage moments I had with the most wonderfully accomplished comedian Andy Ford. He taught me so much. One of the first lessons was, 'David, you must learn to almost never look at the person you're talking to. This is panto!' I will also remember the wonderfully talented female impersonator Ceri Dupree and the most talented singer and musical performer Faye Tozer.

*Lastly, do you have a favourite pantomime?*

I suppose that would have to be *Mother Goose.*

# 1

# ONCE UPON A TIME

## THE EVOLUTION OF PANTOMIME

One of my absolute favourite things about panto is that when you perform in one, you can sense the rich history that you're stepping into, and hear, see and feel the connections it has to other art forms. The pantomimes we go to see today are mostly based on fairy tales – *Jack and the Beanstalk*, *Dick Whittington*, *Cinderella* – or fantastical narratives like *Peter Pan*, and that is a large part of their fabulous, escapist magic. The form's own roots, however, are very real and, fittingly for a form of entertainment that speaks to a broad demographic, they reach far and wide. In fact they go back to ancient Greece, as far as we know – the word 'pantomime' comes from the Greek, meaning 'imitator of all', and originally referred to individual performers who used mime and physicality to entertain an audience, sometimes with a musical backing.

Here, however, I'll mainly be looking at its more recent history, where you can see clear hints of today's pantomime template emerging. I'm not a historian, so this is a look at some of the genres that have shaped pantomime as I've learned about them over the past couple of decades working in it. It's neither a comprehensive nor an academic guide to pantomime's roots – and if you do want to read that, I'd highly recommend Jeffrey Richards's excellent *The Golden Age of Pantomime*, on the Victorian era of panto, or *The Pantomime Life of Joseph Grimaldi* by Andrew McConnell Stott, which takes a more focused look at one of its greatest stars.

The longer I've performed in them, the more pantomime's rich influences have revealed themselves. One of my favourite quotes about pantomime comes from the brilliant Simon Callow, and speaks to the nebulous nature of the genre, but also to its heart: 'There has always been a certain uncertainty about what panto is – which continues to the present day. Above all, it's about the relationship between the actors and the audience.'[1]

The genre is a little like a sponge, soaking up influences of the various eras it has emerged from, survived through and thrived in, expanding, but never losing its essence or shape. It is, at its core, a form of art and entertainment meant for the masses, and it's notable that all the influences that have shaped it have been similarly populist, designed for a cross-section of society.

## MISCHIEF, ROLE REVERSAL AND . . . SHAKESPEARE

A key part of that mass appeal – and pantomime's greatest draw, for me – is its mischievous subversion of power dynamics. The good and usually poor character (think Cinderella, Aladdin, Snow White) succeeds in the end, winning out over the wicked and usually rich character (think the Evil Stepmother, Jafar, the Evil Queen), i.e. the one I normally play. In real life, it's vanishingly rare for the poor to succeed when pitted against the rich, or for anyone to have a true rags-to-riches trajectory. Seeing it up on stage is like wish fulfilment. Additionally, the audience is given the power to shape the play along the way: to shout, cheer and boo the players, and get involved themselves – sometimes literally being invited up on stage to join in.

This combination of subversiveness and emotional release can be traced back to ancient times. The satyr plays, which were performed in the aftermath of three tragedy plays, emerged in ancient Greece, and in them we can see early hints of the raucous and cathartic qualities of pantomime. The main characteristics of the satyr play included a chorus of satyrs (which were mythical half-man, half-beast creatures), fancy costumes, lots of heavy innuendo and jokes of a lewd nature – all of which have a trace in today's pantomimes, from naughty double entendre to the role of the audience commenting on the action of the play.

Similarly bacchanalian antics to those of the satyr plays could be found in ancient Rome in the guise of the festival of Saturnalia, which celebrated the rule of the god Saturn. Saturn's mythical reign was one of unmatched prosperity and peace, so the festivities were suitably merry. As part of the Saturnalia celebrations, social roles were reversed for the day, with a 'King of Saturnalia' being elected to oversee the merriment.

This brief handing over of power to those who have none also took place in Tudor England, when there was something called the 'Day of Misrule', where the lord of the land and his subjects swapped places. Instead of a King of Saturnalia, there was a 'Lord of Misrule' who was elected to supervise proceedings. This tradition was eventually quashed, most likely through a joy-killing double whammy of the rise of Puritanism and jumpy rulers becoming increasingly worried about their subjects getting a hankering for a longer-term switching of roles.

I suppose audience voting in TV talent shows like *Strictly Come Dancing* introduces a bit of that feeling of misrule – we judges might bring expertise to our roles and give our verdict on which acts should have the highest and lowest scores each week, but the audience can upend our decision based on which acts they personally prefer.

And there's a strong element of misrule alive and well in pantomime today. It's a clear form of catharsis for the audience, particularly in difficult times. People who might be struggling at work or at home are able, just for a couple of hours, to come and shout at the 'baddies', and laugh at jokes about the government or a local business owner they don't like. If something kicks off in the country – say the price of groceries is going through the roof, or there's a political scandal, for example – pantomime scriptwriters or the comics performing in the shows will inevitably do a gag about it. Actor Christopher Biggins is famous for dropping in jokes about very current news. That targeted sort of comedy is so important – it allows people to laugh and take their frustrations out on a clearly designated villain. I should know – I get the loudest boos!

Conversely, misrule can also be used as a way for bosses to show their appreciation for their staff: theatrical producer Cameron Mackintosh, who had a panto at his house every year, had the people who work for his company play the lords and ladies, while Cameron himself was there playing the lower-class characters, typically with a broomstick, sweeping the floor and doing what he was told.

The most famous playwright to weave misrule into a number of his works was the Bard himself, William Shakespeare – *Twelfth Night* being the most obvious example. Twelfth Night was once an annual festival in England, and a particularly ripe occasion for misrule. King Henry VIII, not a man known to shy away from a touch of debauchery and revelry, was said to have once dressed himself and his noblemen as Robin Hood and his Merry Men (or at least similar outlaw figures) and gone into the queen's chambers in this disguise.[2] What a wag.

The most visibly evident form of misrule in Shakespeare's plays is their gender subversion. In Shakespeare's time, of course, men played all the women's roles, because women weren't allowed on stage, so cross-dressing was essential if women were to be depicted at all. Even so, we see Shakespeare playing on this theme within his plays, beyond the necessity of male actors playing women – notably in the roles of Viola/Cesario in *Twelfth Night* and Rosalind/Ganymede in *As You Like It*, where the female characters pretend to be men. Although this cross-dressing is ostensibly a way for those characters to survive life-threatening circumstances – shipwreck in a foreign land for Viola and banishment by her uncle for Rosalind – the gender swap allows them to explore power dynamics with their male counterparts. And inevitably to cause no end of chaos as they do so.

There are other things in common between Shakespeare's plays and pantomime, such as the 'stock' characters that recur across multiple works – the jester, the hero, the villain, the comedic duo and so on. Shakespeare's brilliant wordplay and multi-layered jokes, deliberately designed to appeal to young and old alike, are also carried on in panto, as are the references to contemporary events and the actors speaking directly to the audience.

When you think about it, back when Shakespeare was writing and his plays were put on at the Globe, in the 1590s and early 1600s, interaction between actors and audience was normal. We're so used to theatres being hushed today, with the audience silent except in very clearly demarcated moments. From everything we know about that time, however, audiences were pretty raucous. Theatre back then was a form of popular entertainment, and today, pantomime is one of the few types of performance that can still confidently claim to be that.

I really don't believe it's a coincidence that panto attracts Shakespearean actors today. Nor does Stephenson Ardern-Sodje, who played the prince in last year's Theatre Royal Nottingham production of *Cinderella* alongside me, and who draws direct parallels between Shakespeare and pantomime:

*I've been to the Globe and seen Shakespeare plays performed there. The prose is delivered to the groundlings in the stalls, and the poetry is delivered up high to the people in the pricier seats. It's ****ing panto! It's funny when people are elitist about pantomime. It has run for hundreds of years. There is value in it, culturally and economically, so it's snobbish as a performer to take an attitude of, 'I don't think there's anything good about panto.' Well, a million people every year disagree with you.*

And so do some pretty formidable Shakespearean actors, such as Sir Ian McKellen, Sir Patrick Stewart, Sir David Suchet, Simon Callow and Dame Judi Dench, all of whom have graced the boards of panto. It's easy to see why: they can play the characters to their full worth, artistically. And they have more freedom than they do in Shakespeare plays to change words and improvise, which is always a breath of fresh air for us performers.

## AN ITALIAN DETOUR

Improvisation is a strand of pantomime that leads us to another of the genre's ancestors, one that reached its peak of popularity at a similar time to when Shakespeare was writing. While it seems as quintessentially British as the *Carry On* films and fish and chips, pantomime's clearest forebear is arguably found in Italy and the art form of *commedia dell'arte* – or in English, 'comedy of professional artists'. The *commedia dell'arte*, which thrived from the sixteenth through to the eighteenth century, was one of the first things I learned about panto's history when I started performing in it regularly. Improvisation was one of its defining characteristics, along with stock characters, gender-role subversion, jokes relating to current affairs (sound familiar?) and rehearsed comic routines called *lazzi*. A key difference between *commedia* and panto, however, was that the former was performed masked. Masks would have made the gender swapping a little easier for performers, I guess. I'd spend a lot less time getting my make-up ready if I just had to wear a mask, that's for sure!

Although *commedia dell'arte* actors usually specialised in a particular role, much like in today's pantomime, the ability to perform multiple roles came in handy, and the same actor could often play two or more parts within the same production. Obviously this 'multi-roling' is a good way to keep costs down, particularly for local or smaller productions, and can also be used for comedic effect.*

* Another spin-off from *commedia dell'arte* shares a number of characteristics with pantomime: Punch and Judy, derived from the *commedia* character of Pulcinella. Like

A major shift that *commedia dell'arte* brought in was having women on stage, at a time when they were still banned in English theatre. It's likely that this helped change the policy in England soon after the restoration of the monarchy in 1660. That year, Margaret Hughes became the first woman to appear on the English stage, as Desdemona in *Othello*, and in 1662 a royal warrant officially sanctioned female performers, paving the way for figures such as Nell Gwyn, the most celebrated actress of the period and the mistress of King Charles II. It seems bizarre to think that until this point women weren't allowed on stage – and that it would need royal approval to overrule that. It makes you wonder what the authorities back then were so afraid would happen.

Even in the Victorian era – by which time women had been allowed to perform on stage for a couple of centuries – the idea of female actors impersonating men was seen as risqué. This gender-swapping act found a popular home, however, in music halls, which mainly put on bawdy musical and comedic entertainment, and encouraged audience participation, making them the perfect venues for staging pantomimes. Music hall made stars of women who specialised in male impersonation, such as Merseyside-born actress Hetty King, who went on to appear in pantomime, initially as the titular hero in *Dick Whittington* in 1905 and from then onwards playing 'Principal Boy' roles (more on the stock roles of pantomime later). Other famous

panto, this puppet show features subversion of social norms, anti-authority behaviour and lots of audience interaction. Punch and Judy's cruelty is more explicit than we ever see in pantomime, but the pleasure that panto villains take in humiliating and inflicting pain on their sidekicks is very much in the same tradition.

male impersonators included Nelly Power and Vesta Tilley, the latter of whom was one of the highest-earning women in England during the Victorian and Edwardian eras, thanks not only to her commanding high performance fees, but also to the licensing deals she secured to have her name on a variety of products, from socks to cigars.[3] And we think celebs appearing in ads is a new thing!

Another aspect of *commedia dell'arte* that travelled over from Italy into English theatre, and that played a pivotal part in shaping pantomime, was the Harlequin figure. Today, younger generations might have a rough idea of the look of the Harlequin because of the character Harley Quinn in the *Batman* DC Comics universe, whose dress and make-up is designed as a simplified version of the traditional, *commedia dell'arte*-derived Harlequin costume.

The original Harlequin ('Arlecchino'), however, was a servant character, whose initial role was primarily to bring comic relief, wooing his love interest, Columbine, through physical acrobatics and cunning schemes (some of these traits remain in the character of Harley Quinn – the Joker's erstwhile companion, albeit one entirely in his thrall). The famous Harlequin outfit of multicoloured diamonds supposedly originated from the fact he was too poor to afford clothes and so had to stitch pieces of fabric together instead. He was a mischievous troublemaker who enjoyed causing havoc, a bit like Bruno Tonioli and Anton Du Beke on *Strictly*.

Actor Tristano Martinelli's success in the role of Harlequin, which he performed in Italy, France and beyond, from the 1580s until his death in 1630, brought him considerable success and fame during his life and ensured the Harlequin character's continued popularity in the *commedia* after his death. He was so successful, in fact, that he was known as 'Dominus Arlecchinorum', or Master of Harlequins. It's around this time, in the mid- to late sixteenth century, that you see wordplay becoming more important, too, in the art form in general and particularly within this role. In *commedia dell'arte* performances prior to Martinelli's influence, the main comic role was primarily a physical character, demonstrating his playfulness and mischief through acrobatics and mime. Martinelli's Harlequin, however, was no longer simply the 'fool', but rather a quick-thinking servant capable of outwitting his masters.

So beloved was the Harlequin, in fact, that he had his own spin-off show in the form of the harlequinade, a type of comic play found in English theatre from the seventeenth century onwards. Another actor, John Rich, made his name in the role of Harlequin in the eighteenth century, and in this period, the English Harlequin moved away from the comedic, slapstick character of its Italian ancestor, leaving that to the 'clown' figure, and morphed into a romantic lead. It is Rich who is largely credited with moving the harlequinade into the form we think of as pantomime today, with his performances at Covent Garden Theatre between 1732 and 1760. It was primarily due to the success of John Rich's performances that actor David Garrick began to stage his own pantomimes at the Theatre Royal, Drury Lane, despite supposedly looking down his nose at the genre.

The term 'pantomime', rather than 'harlequinade', is in fact thought to have first been used in England even earlier than this – in 1717, to be precise, by John Weaver, a ballet dancer and choreographer, for his production *The Loves of Mars and Venus*. Although his productions were closer to what we might nowadays call theatrical ballet, he used elements of the *commedia*, including the Harlequin, in his performances, and is consequently known as the father of English pantomime.

There was a shift away from the Harlequin as the main figure in pantomime by the nineteenth century, particularly as the remarkable skill of actor Joseph Grimaldi – who found fans in luminaries such as Charles Dickens and William Hazlitt[4] – brought the clown character to the fore. With his gymnastic feats and his extraordinarily expressive face, he became the star of the harlequinades, and inevitably scripts began to centre him over the Harlequin. Grimaldi was famous for appearing in two shows a night, at different theatres, and having to dash from one to the other between performances. I thought we had it tough today!

Harlequins are no longer a regular feature of pantomime productions, but thankfully there are still people continuing to keep the role, and other aspects of *commedia dell'arte*, alive. Ben-Jamin Newham is artistic director and principal actor of Fools in Progress, a theatre company specialising in *commedia dell'arte* in Australia. At the very young age of sixteen, he trained in the form for five months in Italy under the tutelage of Antonio Fava, *maestro* of *commedia dell'arte*. Today he has risen through the ranks of Fools in Progress to become its artistic director. While Ben-Jamin performs many of the roles in *commedia*, he is especially celebrated for his performances in the servant or Harlequin role. It's invigorating and reassuring to see new generations picking up the torch and continuing to find inspiration in such old art forms.

A key turning point in pantomime's history was the Theatres Act of 1843, which allowed theatres without a royal patent to put on spoken-word-only plays. Pantomimes could be performed in spaces like music halls without having to be quite so reliant on music and spectacle as before the decree. Suddenly, the sort of wordplay that we're used to in pantomime today was able to flourish in venues beyond those like Drury Lane that had a royal patent, making pantomime increasingly appealing for actors and audiences alike. During the music hall era, which lasted roughly from the 1830s to 1918, the genre proved so popular that prominent actors were increasingly drawn to perform in its main roles. Impresario Sir Augustus Harris, who took over management of the Drury Lane theatre in 1879 at the tender age of twenty-seven, while not necessarily the first producer to cast star actors in his shows, is nevertheless credited with making it more of a consistent feature, particularly of his Christmas pantomime shows. He understood the appeal of a glitzy name and was well rewarded for his casting choices, with his shows often running well beyond the Christmas season through to spring.

That tradition never left the genre, and happily for me, celebs still get asked to perform in pantos every year. I visit a lot of theatres with my one-man show – usually up to fifty venues each year – and I see old posters in the dressing rooms from times gone by, especially the 1920s, 1930s and 1940s. The people headlining panto on the posters are actors who had become celebrated for their work in plays or musical comedy or variety acts, and it's strange to see their faces, which must have been so well known in their day, but now mean little or nothing to us.

The use of variety-style 'acts' is another hangover from both music hall shows and *commedia dell'arte* that continues to show up in pantomime now. While clowns have definitely fallen out of favour in pantos today – I'm not sure if that's because of one too many horror movies with clown serial killers in them – and the Harlequin is very much relegated to the past, there's usually a comedian, an acrobatic or dance troupe or a performing animal in pantomimes, the sort of acts that are still popular on shows like *Britain's Got Talent*. It's like going to see twenty acts rolled into one. That's one of the wonderful things about pantomime: the more you look into the various aspects that make it up, the more you see how it takes old forms and presents them in a contemporary way that resonates with audiences, constantly renewing itself.

Max Fulham, a scriptwriter, ventriloquist and actor in pantomime, is particularly celebrated for providing the 'act' or 'routine' section of the pantos he performs in. While those parts of a pantomime might seem almost off the cuff, because they're performed with such ease – and usually as moments of high comedy – he points out that that's mostly not the case.

*I really do consider pantomime a year-round job: I start thinking about the next one pretty much as soon the curtain falls on the last. I try to get my hands on the first draft of a script as soon as I can in the year so I can see what bits are needed from me and get to work. Sometimes it will be a case of warming up existing routines if it isn't a show or venue I have done before, but for new routines it can take a lot longer.*

Max confesses to being something of a nerd when it comes to theatre and comedy performance, and he has really taken the time to understand the rich history of pantomime:

*From the moment I became interested in comedy and ventriloquism I have always been a fan of the old stuff. Having researched various music hall performers, because I'm a silly little comedy nerd, I would often see pantomimes mentioned so I was aware that variety played a huge part in pantomime's history. I feel very lucky to be continuing that tradition of the speciality act and bringing it to modern audiences. It is amazing to be following in the footsteps of many ventriloquists before me, including the incredible Dawson Chance who performed in pantomimes for forty-seven years and who I am now lucky enough to call a good friend.*

Like Dawson Chance, Max's act is usually ventriloquism, but there is a whole range of performance types that get called on to provide this element of the show. During the 2025 Christmas season, for example, Ashley Banjo and the Diversity dance group, who found fame on *Britain's Got Talent* in 2009, performed in *Robin Hood* at the New Wimbledon Theatre alongside comic-magician Pete Firman, who has a four-million-strong social media following and appears regularly on TV.

Sometimes the 'act' goes on to top the bill – a brilliant example of this is father-and-son duo Clive Webb and Danny Adams. Danny has a show on CBBC called *Danny & Mick*, performing with his brother, Mick Potts. Clive started out playing drums in a pop band, but got his real performing chops when he joined the circus – the famous Robert Brothers Circus, to be exact – initially as a drummer, before becoming a clown. The two have used their skills in comedy and the circus to perfect their pantomime act, making the Theatre Royal in Newcastle their home. They've sold out tickets to audiences every year, who can't get enough of them. Having begun in panto as a support act to Jill Halfpenny, they ultimately proved so popular that they topped the bill and never looked back.

Just like the *commedia* acts of centuries ago, these guys bring their fans to panto and add a bit of razzle-dazzle to the storyline with their extraordinary skills. Unlike in variety shows, however, those aspects of dance, magic and comedy are used to help shape the story and are woven into the plot.

## FAIRY STORIES AND CHANGING WITH THE TIMES

One of the key aspects of contemporary pantomime only really emerged in the mid- to late nineteenth century: the fairy-tale story. A British playwright called J. R. Planché wrote or in some way worked on 176 plays during his lifetime. He dabbled in a range of forms, but the one we're interested in as it relates to pantomime is the 'extravaganza', which he was responsible for popularising. Like pantomime as we know it today, extravaganzas featured music and dance – and burlesque. We now associate burlesque with stylishly racy performances – think Dita von Teese – but it was originally a form of satire, its name derived from the Italian *burlesco*, meaning a joke or mockery – which ties in nicely with the 'imitation' meaning of pantomime; satire is a comic rendition of a serious issue. At some point, Planché felt burlesque was becoming stale, and keen to freshen things up, he turned to the seventeenth-century French fairy tales of Madame d'Aulnoy for inspiration – who borrowed heavily from older sources, including oral folk tales. Like the original Brothers Grimm stories, to which we'll come in the next chapter, these fairy stories were useful vehicles for social satire through entertaining tales. In total Planché wrote twenty-three fairy extravaganzas, including *Beauty and the Beast* and *The Sleeping Beauty in the Wood*. In these plays, you can see the current shape of pantomime begin to emerge.

Another playwright moving within the same bohemian circles as Planché was one Edward Litt Laman Blanchard, whose work was heavily influenced by Planché's extravaganzas. From 1852, Blanchard wrote pantomimes for the Drury Lane theatre, with fairy tales and mythical stories becoming a consistent inspiration for scripts, many of which you'd expect to see performed today – *Aladdin*, *Cinderella*, *Beauty and the Beast* – and others that are now more likely to remain in the pages of children's books, from *Little Jack Horner* to *Tom Thumb*.

The appeal of fairy stories, and how they have become such an essential part of pantomime scripts today, is perhaps obvious – they're simple stories, mostly with reassuring endings: the villains get their comeuppance, and the heroes and heroines either save the day or are saved. However, there is a moralising element in many fairy stories that some in Planché and Blanchard's time pushed back against, not appreciating the feeling of being lectured. While it's understandable not to want to have morality preached to you, the good-triumphing-over-bad aspect of fairy tales is an element that's probably helped pantomime stand the test of time: it is family entertainment, after all, where many young children have their first experience of theatre; and parents know the content is safe and promoting good values in a fun way.

Though pantomime hasn't really travelled beyond British shores since it settled into the form we recognise today, there is one country that has taken the genre and reimagined it, using the folk tales of its heritage rather than fairy tales as the basis for plots. The Little Theatre Movement of Jamaica, founded in 1941 by Henry Fowler and Greta Burke, began that very same year to put on a Christmas pantomime. In its initial years, the company mostly put on the fairy tale-derived pantos of British tradition, although as early as 1943 they performed the first Jamaican pantomime proper, *Soliday and the Wicked Bird*. Through the 1950s and 1960s, the Jamaican National Pantomime's output began to be solely derived from traditional Jamaican folk tales and aspects of Jamaican cultural history thanks to actor and comedian Ranny Williams and poet, actor, author and folklorist Louise Bennett. The use of traditional tales helped to preserve these elements of the nation's heritage. The dance pieces were also used to weave in national customs, though these have shifted over time to reflect cultural trends.[5] Today, the Jamaican National Pantomime is thriving, most recently with the 2025–6 production of *Big Yaad Vibes*, staged at the Little Theatre, which opened – as is traditional – on Boxing Day.

This shift towards more recent trends is also true of British pantomime's choreography, which has changed significantly since the early days of the genre. Back in the eighteenth century, you would have had a ballet troupe performing in pantomime, hard as that is to imagine now. As a result, traditional choreography for pantomime is not too dissimilar to classical ballet: an even-numbered group of dancers, and the use of formations – generally diagonals from the centre to introduce a star, and crossovers upstage, with traditional walkdowns. This seems to have stemmed from ballet dancers appearing in operas from the seventeenth century onwards. Today we don't think of opera as mainstream or mass-market, but it was in the past, particularly in the Romantic era (*c.* 1830–1900). It's only more recently that it has been deemed somehow elite, or 'high' art.

While dancers aren't a feature of opera so much now, they were used to entertain opera audiences in the 1800s and early 1900s. This is said to have stemmed from King Louis XIV of France insisting that ballet be integrated into the Italian operas that were being put on in France during his reign. These dance interludes were usually placed in the first or second acts. By the 1800s, the dance element had been relegated to the intervals between acts by Italian practitioners, although the French 'grand opera' tradition still demanded that a ballet be performed within the first couple of acts. Giuseppe Verdi, the composer of the operas *La Traviata*, *Rigoletto* and *Aida*, among others, was made to put ballet into his operatic works between acts, thanks to the Parisian opera house regulations, by all accounts against his will. Presumably he thought it distracted from his beautiful music. Giacomo Puccini, whose operatic compositions included *La Bohème*, *Madama Butterfly* and *Tosca*, meanwhile, seems to have embraced it more enthusiastically. It is most likely this use of ballet alongside the theatrical music of opera that has led to dance being incorporated into both musicals and pantomime today. I wonder what Timothée Chalamet would make of that . . .

Thanks to MTV and the explosion of music videos in the 1980s, the music and dance in pantomimes rapidly changed to become more up to date with current trends. If you go to your local pantomime today, you'll inevitably hear songs by chart-topping artists like Dua Lipa or Taylor Swift. There's a music licence that covers venues for the use of pop songs in pantomime productions and allows us to use even the biggest hit songs in our shows. Words often get changed to link the songs back to the story of the particular pantomime, or to make jokes, like 'All I Want for Christmas Is Youth' being sung by the Fairy Godmother. It makes sense to have current pop songs in the shows, so they don't feel old hat. Some songs cross generations, of course. I sang a Blondie number when I played Hook – 'One Way or Another' – and that song came out in 1978, but then it was covered by One Direction for Comic Relief's Red Nose Day in 2013, and a whole new audience discovered it. All the kids knew the One Direction version and their parents knew the Blondie original, so the entire family could sing along together.

When it comes to pantomimes being performed at Christmas, the reason certainly doesn't lie within the stories being performed. American actor and singer Christina Bianco, who played the Fairy Godmother in *Cinderella* with me in Nottingham in 2025, recalls being baffled by the lack of any reference to Christmas when she went to see pantomimes for the first time:

*I thought, wow, they're so clever and they're so naughty and so joyous and so sweet. But yes, it was quite a shock to me that there was no Christmas element. I kept waiting for connection to Christmas because I knew they were only put on at Christmas, until a friend pointed out that they weren't Christmas stories.*

One possible origin for the Christmas timing of pantomime performances lies in the medieval form of mummers' plays. These shared some traits with pantomime, for instance a 'good' character defeating the 'bad' – whether St George against the Dragon or Robin Hood against the Sheriff of Nottingham – the use of comedy, and a dance element. They were traditionally performed around Christmas time and it's possible this was carried over into pantomime. What we know for sure is that David Garrick, who was responsible for the Harlequin becoming a sharp-tongued role, spotted the dual function of scheduling pantomime for Christmas: it ensured that it would be deemed comparatively superficial fun, and not judged as serious 'art', but whatever his personal thoughts, it was also undeniably popular and an excellent revenue driver. By the Victorian era, while the bawdy music hall influence was evident in pantomime, the genre had also established itself as a form of family entertainment, and the Christmas timing was cemented.

Throughout its history, pantomime has combined art and entertainment in an extraordinary way, and I truly see it as an art form on a par with Shakespeare's plays for sheer ingenuity. Actors who perform regularly in pantomime today operate as proper old-fashioned troupes – having a group of people who know and are at ease with each other means you can easily pick up for another actor if there are any problems on the night, or help each other out with cues if you've been put off by distractions from the audience. This approach goes all the way back to Italy and the *commedia dell'arte* – these troupes were referred to then as *compagnie comiche* – and it ensures a reliable standard of performance.

The fact that pantomime is more popular than ever is testament to its enduring appeal – and it's why I'm still turning out to perform in panto every year. While various aspects of it have changed, as it morphed from its early roots in other art forms to the very distinctive shape it takes today, it has somehow retained its key elements and core charm, while managing to evolve and remain relevant.

## THE PUNTERS

One of the things that both baffles and irritates me, and that comes up time and again in the course of my conversations with other panto professionals throughout this book, is the snobbery towards the genre. I've been open about the fact I didn't like panto for a long time, thinking it was just poor-quality theatre, but that was largely because of the way it was talked about.

There's no question that part of the attitude towards pantomime stems from class. Class *is* present in Australia, but it's not such an obvious thing as it is here in the UK, where there is still a lot of sneering if you don't like the 'right' sort of art. I'm just so glad that I was asked to get involved in panto and was able to learn what a genius thing it actually is. And that I get to shout about it in a book like this.

The people who are *never* snobbish about panto are the people who come out to see it each year, and get the absolute joy and brilliance of it. So I thought it was worth taking a look back at how audiences have changed since the times of *commedia dell'arte* and the early days of pantomime, and how the elitism around panto can be traced to the demographics of the people who have been drawn to it over the centuries.

Chiara D'Anna, director, actor and *commedia dell'arte* specialist, writes incredibly insightfully not just about the performers of *commedia* but also about the audience. What made *commedia* different to the pantomime of today, she observes, is that the notion of the 'Fourth Wall' was simply not a thing then: 'The actors and audiences of Commedia dell'Arte were interacting . . . Personally, I believe Commedia is performed with an audience, not for an audience . . . In a Commedia performance, everything is directed to and shared with the audience. Every gaze, action, and line.'[6]

I love this idea of the audience being even more integral to performances than we already think of them being in pantomime. *Commedia* is sometimes thought of as street performance, but it was performed inside as well, and its audience was made up of all walks of society, from the general public to the aristocracy. Its influence is impossible to overstate, and its blend of improvisation with, increasingly over time, the use of witty dialogue paved the way for the lauded playwrights of subsequent generations, from Carlo Goldoni (who is credited with making *commedia* a fully scripted form) to the French playwright Molière, along with British playwrights William Shakespeare and Ben Jonson.

The audience for Shakespeare's plays during his lifetime is often noted as having been a similarly broad cross-section of society to the audience for *commedia*. While a lot of us think of Shakespeare's plays as something we had to study for exams as kids, back when he was alive they were very much storytelling to be experienced and heard, as opposed to the written form we tend to first encounter them in today. It's sad and a little odd to think how Shakespeare's work has become synonymous with elitism and opaque language, when in his time, his plays were performed to a primarily illiterate audience, their themes reflecting the issues faced by servants and other ordinary people as much as the wealthy. With audiences ranging from the poor ('groundlings', who could pay a penny to stand in the open-air yard), through the middle classes and nobility, this was art and entertainment for everyone.

Which is precisely what pantomime is, too. So when did it become something to be sneered at? While the Victorian era was certainly not the first period in which social elitism impacted the art form (its foreign origins and the increasing significance of the clown role meant panto had many critics in the Georgian era, for example), I *suspect* the answer lies mostly in the Victorians' special brand of moral puritanism. Or perhaps more accurately the *appearance* of moral purity, which became a way in which the middle classes could distinguish themselves from the lower.

As industrialisation brought more and more workers from the countryside into the cities, social unrest unsurprisingly came along with them, as the gap between the haves and the have-nots was all too clear. I'm not a historian, as I've said, but

I don't think you need to be to see how the embracing of very strict moral codes, gender norms and increasingly distinct expectations of the social classes was a way for the better-offs to protect their place in society in the face of very rapid change.

Of course it's a total nonsense to think that the middle and upper classes weren't indulging in as much filth and bawdiness as the working classes, if not more so. They just did it behind closed doors. Meanwhile, variety acts and music halls, which evolved from tavern entertainment, were public amusements that were seen as being squarely for the working classes. Music hall performances in particular were usually raucous, a mix of comedy, dance and other variety acts. While women were encouraged to attend as a civilising influence on their partners by Charles Morton (who you'll hear more about in Chapter 5) in his Canterbury Hall venue in Lambeth, these were male-dominated audiences for the most part. And it's fair to say the increasingly frequent appearance of prostitutes touting their wares in the aisles during shows didn't help the reputation of these new music halls as dens of iniquity.

Charles Dickens Jr, whose father had so admired the pantomime performances of Joseph Grimaldi, weighed in on the influence of music halls on the genre, declaring in 1896: 'Then came the deluge, the floodgates of the music hall were opened, and all that was agreeable about the "good comic pantomime" was drained out.'[7] The clear influence of music hall entertainment on the development of pantomime almost inevitably contributed to panto being associated with the lower classes.

As we moved into the 1900s, thankfully there was something of a rejection of the moral purity of the Victorian era, which meant that the middle classes were less afraid of being seen as *déclassé* if they laughed at slapstick comedy, double entendres or – heaven forbid – performers in drag.

The Second World War led to theatre closures and rationing, so performances were harder to stage in those years. Nevertheless, pantomime remained a wonderful escape from the grim realities of wartime life, and drew from radio talent – some of the biggest celebrities of the time – for the starring roles. Even royalty got in on the act, with Princesses Elizabeth and Margaret performing in pantomimes at the Royal School of Windsor.[8] So much for *déclassé*: that's positively aspirational!

With celebrity pop and TV stars becoming increasingly involved in the world of panto in the 1950s and 1960s, there was a significant commercialisation of the genre, which required greater professionalism and slick production values. But somewhere in the late twentieth century, a slide in standards led to a reversion to the snobbery of old. Throughout the 1970s and 1980s, there came the rise of a more 'blue' form of pantomime, with much more smuttiness and noticeably lazy jokes becoming a common feature of productions. The use of stereotypes and an unpleasant mixture of sexism and racism in the scripts didn't help the perception of pantomime as a 'lower' form of art.

It's been a long slog from there for pantomime to be treated with the level of respect it has today – which is still a wary sort of respect and often only admitted begrudgingly. The professionalisation of pantomime, which we'll look at in Chapter 4, has been a huge factor in turning around the sniffy attitudes towards the genre. Sharp scripts that do the sophisticated work of speaking to a broad spectrum of people, plus attention to the detail of every single aspect of production, means that the pantomimes you see today are of an undeniably high quality, so it's much harder to be snooty about them.

The audiences of today really are from all kinds of backgrounds. If I don't have to shoot off to get some much-needed sleep after a performance, I like to chat to audience members who've stuck around after the show. It's a community, to me, so it's great to hear how people respond to the shows I perform in – and to see who's turning out to see us all. I've performed in towns and cities all across the UK and it's the same wherever I go, from Manchester to Wimbledon, Cardiff to Glasgow. People from every economic class, ethnicity and religion are buying tickets and coming out to enjoy the productions.

Since the late twentieth century, pantomime has become almost like a rite of passage for kids in the UK. It feels like pretty much everyone I meet here went to at least one when they were growing up, or performed in one at school. Michael Harrison, CEO of the Crossroads production company, is no exception:

*I would see pantomimes multiple times as a child. The first ever pantomime I saw was Dana in* Snow White and the Seven Dwarfs *and I was hooked. In fact, I can remember one particular year* Jack and the Beanstalk *was on at Newcastle's Theatre Royal, starring Little and Large, and I went to see every performance in Christmas week – which was twelve times!*

It really does hook people. Ask friends and colleagues about their first experience of panto. We've all got our own origin story in the genre!

Its near-universality in the country is possibly one of the reasons pantomime gets looked down on; perhaps it's easy to take for granted. I'll come on to this shortly, but the sheer financial weight that pantomime carries in ensuring that theatres can stay open all year round, thanks to the incredible revenue it generates during the season, does command a certain amount of respect within the theatre industry – and where it doesn't, it really ought to. It hasn't always been such a reliable way to get bums on seats, but today the shows deliver both artistically and commercially, and that is not something that happens by accident. And I'm glad that although there is a lot of lingering snootiness towards it, that excellence is finally being better acknowledged. Audiences always know what is good, and their turning out in record numbers to see pantomime today says it all.

When I'm performing on stage, I love to think of audiences in the distant past – who would have sat watching a similar show to the one the audience in front of me is seeing – and of the actors whose footsteps I'm following in. It's easy to feel the centuries melt away, and to feel a kinship with those actors and audiences of long ago – and to be grateful that I'm a part of the history that links us all together.

# GUEST STAR

# PAUL CHUCKLE

An icon of children's TV thanks to *ChuckleVision*, which he made and performed in with his late brother Barry, with whom he was also part of a comedy duo, Paul Chuckle has won over new fans in every single decade of his career.

He's become a popular figure on TikTok in recent years and is performing at the National Theatre this year as Mr Boo in *The Rise and Fall of Little Voice* – which is the only thing stopping him getting to a whopping sixty pantomime performances! We've performed in panto together, and it was a delight to chat to him about this fantastic form of theatre we've both come to love so much.

*When did you first get into panto?*

Barry and I won *Opportunity Knocks* in 1967, and someone came and booked us to do *Babes in the Wood* at Malvern Theatre, a very old, small venue. *Babes in the Wood* is one people don't really do any more. Given it's about two criminals preparing to take two kids into the woods and kill them, you can see why! Top of the bill was Sandy Powell, a comedian from Rotherham. He was well known at the time for his catchphrase, 'Can you hear me, Mother?' which was woven into the production.

I've known Nick Thomas who used to own Qdos Entertainment since 1975. He was the winner on a show called *New Faces* in 1975 – aged just fifteen, as a puppeteer. So Barry and I had known him for donkey's years. The first panto we did with him was 1984, I think. Back then it was Nick Thomas

Enterprises, before it became Qdos. We've worked with Qdos, and now Crossroads, ever since.

*Had you always enjoyed pantomime or was it only when you performed in it that you caught the bug?*

I was brought up in show business – Dad was a comedian. He got banned from radio in 1939 for two years for ending a joke with, 'It was smooth as a baby's bottom.' My dad and my elder brothers all performed in pantomimes, so Barry and I were raised surrounded by the genre. Having watched them all performing for years, by the time the two of us got into show business ourselves, we knew every single pantomime there is.

*How have you found pantomime has changed over the years?*

Theoretically, it hasn't changed at all. The stories are the same, the heart of it's the same. There's a lot more wariness about what can and can't be said now – like I said, *Babes in the Wood* just isn't put on any more for that reason. Barry and I were just there for the laughs, and as I see it, as long as people go away at the end of the show laughing, that's all that matters.

It's quite all-singing, all-dancing these days, but I don't do those aspects of it, except for a comedy song at the start.

*You tend to be cast as the funny, likeable character, have you ever had a hankering to cross over to the dark side?*

I like to make people laugh, so I enjoy playing the funny good guy roles. I've never been the baddie, and I've never really wanted to be.

*Are there any panto icons you've enjoyed playing alongside?*

Well, you! Last time we were in panto together I was your husband, Baron Hardup, in *Cinderella*, when you were the Evil Stepmother. You can dance, sing, act and you're very funny. [Stop, you're making me blush, Paul!] But aside from you, I've been lucky enough to work with loads of brilliant people over the years, like Arthur Askey. One of the funniest comedians I've ever worked with was a guy called Stuart Francis. He used to do *Crackerjack* and was known for his 'I could crush a grape' catchphrase.

*Have you got a favourite panto?*

*Aladdin* was always Barry's and my favourite – it's a good story. We usually played the policemen. But it didn't matter what show it was, really, we always had fun. We performed everywhere, from Scotland to Plymouth and the southwest, Birmingham, Sheffield, Bradford and the northeast . . .

*Have you got any advice for people just starting out in pantomime?*

It's incredible fun, but it's also very tiring: it's twelve shows a week over six days and you only get Christmas Day and

New Year's Day off, so it's hard work. It's not an easy thing, but despite that, you have to always give it 100 per cent when you're on stage. There are a lot of people who come into the business, and if the audience is only filling half the venue, they walk through the show thinking, 'What's the point?' But every single one of those people who've come to watch have paid the ticket price, and it's not their fault that the rest of the theatre wasn't packed out. You have to be there to put on the show, so why not give it your all?

It's a very friendly business – of course you get some people who aren't easy to work with, but it's a team sport so anyone who isn't welcoming doesn't tend to stick around long. It really comes over the footlights if the company are all happy and having a good time, and it ensures the audience are too.

# 2

# HAPPILY EVER AFTER

## OUR FAVOURITE PANTOMIMES' ORIGIN STORIES

There are only a handful of stories that get performed in pantomime today, which is convenient since it means we actors don't have to keep learning new plotlines! The same hits draw in the crowds every year, most of which I've been lucky enough to perform in. Thanks to Planché and Blanchard, the most beloved panto scripts today are derived from fairy tales, with romances like *Cinderella*, *Snow White* and *Sleeping Beauty* proving particular favourites, alongside non-love-story classics, such as *Jack and the Beanstalk*.

Like most forms of entertainment, different pantos rise and fall in popularity; old-time favourites like *Babes in the Wood*, *Rapunzel*, *Puss in Boots* and *Dick Whittington* have gone a little out of fashion in recent years, for example. The tastes of children and adults alike inevitably change depending on the world they're living in, and unless the stories are rewritten to be relevant to the moment they're performed in, it's easy for these old tales to feel out of step with the times. And as I've said before, the reason pantomime has survived and thrived through the centuries is because it adapts to the world around it and what is popular at any given moment.

The very crude jokes that littered old performances of *Dick Whittington* and *Puss in Boots* feel a bit tired now, and it's fair to say that producers seem more nervous about putting those particular shows on. The pantomimes that are popular at the moment tend to be less reliant on bawdy humour – and have sharper scripts. I did think that the 2011 animated film of *Puss in Boots* starring Antonio Banderas might have led to a resurgence on stage, but for some reason it didn't cross over.

Being businesspeople as well as creatives, producers will naturally only put on shows that they know people will buy tickets for. The musical *Annie*, for example, is on every couple of years because people love it; they know it. The same is true for the pantomime of *Cinderella*. It's a timeless story that we all grow up with in storybooks and on our screens, and people have always loved a love story.

In such tough economic times, people are understandably hesitant to spend a lot of money on a pantomime that they are not familiar with. They want to be guaranteed an enjoyable show, so producers can't afford to take a risk on something lesser known or old-fashioned, whereas they can be sure with *Cinderella* they'll sell tickets out within the first two months of it being advertised. To make a show sell these days, though, the core essentials are more or less the same as they ever have been: 1) a popular story, 2) great 'acts', whether that's musical performances, comedy, dancing, magic etc., and 3) a celebrity star.

That said, a massive venue like the London Palladium can occasionally take a risk with a more obscure panto, because they have the resources to put on a lavish production, and usually multiple celebrities in their casts. Their audience does tend to skew more adult than most other venues, so the material can be more risqué, too – if you've been to the panto there, you'll know that the jokes are a lot filthier than elsewhere!

A producer can take the bull by the horns and reinvent a show if they have a big budget, but that is very rare. Prior to the Covid pandemic, Michael Harrison was about to stage *Humpty Dumpty* at the Theatre Royal in Newcastle: 'The show was completely designed, with a spectacular set by

Mark Walters, and it's a shame that it never got put on, but I'm hoping we'll do it in the next few years.'

I'm sure it's no coincidence that the most performed pantomimes today are ones that were made into popular Disney films many years ago, which are now streamed into everyone's homes; pretty much every generation that comes to see them on stage will know the stories from the films. *Cinderella*, *Snow White*, *Sleeping Beauty* . . . Whatever your feelings about Disney as a business or brand, the films are perennial classics, available to watch all year round now, thanks to streaming, and it's a rare family that hasn't seen them, so there's a reassuring familiarity when they're performed as pantomimes.

The pantos I'm about to take a closer look at are ones that have been staged for centuries and are also the best loved and most often performed in recent years. These stories almost never fail, because they've been tried and tested over generations. It's interesting to me to see the ways the panto versions of these stories differ from the fairy tales or films – how this particular form of entertainment adds its very own twist to classic tales to win over live audiences afresh every year.

## *CINDERELLA*

This is one of the most popular pantomimes performed today (the second most performed in 2025, according to the Stagely App),[1] along with *Sleeping Beauty* and *Aladdin*. We all know the story, though how many of us know that it stemmed from an ancient Greek folk tale? That story was called *Rhodopis*, named for a Greek slave girl who was said to have lost a sandal, which was snatched up by an eagle and deposited into the lap of a pharaoh. The pharaoh then searched the land to find the owner of the sandal and, on meeting Rhodopis, fell in love with her.

Charles Perrault's fairy tale *Cinderella* from 1697 has the missing footwear element and the servant girl–ruler-of-kingdom love story that we encountered in *Rhodopis*, but his version adds the fairy godmother and the magical glass slippers that we associate with the Cinders story today. The Brothers Grimm's typically dark 1812 reworking – which featured birds that help Cinders throughout the story, pecking the ugly stepsisters' eyes out as a punishment for their treatment of her – kept the story in the public imagination. The Disney animated film of 1950, with Cinderella's powder-blue ballgown and hairband, cemented it as a classic.

The panto version deviates a little from Perrault's original Cinders story. Poor, downtrodden Cinderella lives a life of drudgery, bullied by her wicked stepmother and stepsisters and made to do all the chores: that much is the same. In the pantomime, however, while Cinderella's father is still the spineless man of the fairy tale, he is not a wealthy nobleman as in the original but has instead fallen into financial difficulty, and in a nice bit of nominative determinism is called Baron Hardup of Hardup Hall. Consequently, the Evil Stepmother is set on marrying one of her two daughters off to the prince and returning to the life of luxury they once enjoyed.

Another departure from the original fairy tale – and indeed the Disney film – is the comic character of Buttons. Introduced to the story in 1860 by Gioachino Rossini in his opera of

*Cinderella*, Buttons is a male servant working in the household, his name deriving from that given to the young male servants of the time who wore a particular style of uniform with gilt buttons. He is a saving grace for Cinderella, the one she can always rely on, although she is blissfully unaware that he has an epic crush on her. It's a rare moment for the comic role in a pantomime to have a romantic storyline – albeit an unrequited one.

Meanwhile, Prince Charming wishes to meet a girl on his own terms, not just someone desperate to snag a prince. He and his manservant, Dandini – another addition to the fairy tale that Rossini put into his opera and that has been carried into pantomime – swap clothes and as the prince wanders through the forest/wood (the location varies, depending on the production), pretending to be an ordinary citizen, he meets Cinderella, instantly falling for her. They part ways before he is able to ask her name, however, and in an act of spectacular overkill for someone he's just met, the prince sends out a kingdom-wide invite to a ball, thrown solely in order to find the mysterious beauty.

An invite goes to the Hardup household, but the Baroness rips up Cinderella's ticket, forcing her to stay behind. A constant in fairy tale, Disney film and ballet versions of *Cinderella*, the Fairy Godmother saves the day (in Rossini's opera this character is a mentor or tutor). She delivers that immortal line, 'You *shall* go to the ball!' – then magics up a gorgeous gown from Cinderella's rags, a coach from a pumpkin and horses from mice, and in the pantomime, gives Buttons a fairy-dust transformation, turning him into a coachman (in the Disney film, the coachman is a rat, her footmen lizards). The famous glass slippers are conjured out of pure magic by the Fairy Godmother, so do not have an original form to be transformed back into.

Cinders makes it to the ball, the prince is bedazzled anew, but before the clock strikes midnight, she must leave or risk her dress, horses, carriage and footman turning back into their more prosaic selves. While she makes it out of the ball in the nick of time to avoid being seen in rags, she is too late to catch a ride in her magical carriage before it is transformed back into a pumpkin and must flee home on foot – famously losing a glass slipper in the process.

I'm sure you all know the ending: the next day, the prince and Dandini go in search of the beautiful girl from the ball, clutching the glass slipper she left as she ran away and visiting every house in the land to track Cinderella down. Every house, including Hardup Hall. Despite the evil Baroness's determination to hide Cinderella, and the wicked stepsisters trying everything they possibly can to ram their grotesque feet into the slipper, they cannot make it fit. Finally, Cinderella is called to try on the slipper and it slides on effortlessly, proving her to be the woman of the prince's dreams.

Pantomime productions often adapt the character roles to suit the actors playing them, so there might be a high-camp Baroness Hardup, if the role is played in drag – which I've now done twice – or a bumbling Baron Hardup, if played by a comedy actor. And keeping the form's variety show/music hall roots alive, celebrities' talents are woven in – if they are known for their magic skills, for example, this might be incorporated into the role of Buttons, as he tries to impress Cinderella with his tricks. In the 2025 production of *Cinderella* that I was in, our

Fairy Godmother was played by the singer and impressionist Christina Bianco, who is extraordinary at vocal impressions, so virtuoso trills from Christina Aguilera, Adele and Cher songs were included in her role.

Along with the evolutionary tweaks that have been made over time to keep it relevant, there's a reason *Cinderella* is still performed after 300 years and works in all these different forms – from fairy tale to opera, to pantomime, to Disney film. Yes, it's old, but it's not outdated, because it still has meaning that resonates with people of all ages. We still have a class system today and there's nothing frivolous about it; it's a matter of life and death. *Cinderella* is about being rich or being poor. It's about greed and, looked at with a particularly jaded eye, it's about the fact that, for the poor to become rich, it's usually down to one-in-a-million odds of luck falling in their favour. And that's why we all cheer for Cinderella: we don't really care about the prince; it's the rags-to-riches story we want to see.

## *SNOW WHITE*

Disney movies really do help keep certain stories popular. Even if you have never read the fairy story of *Snow White and the Seven Dwarfs*, popularised in written form by the Brothers Grimm, you will almost certainly have seen the Disney version of it on TV at some point in your childhood. Surprisingly, the bit in the Brothers Grimm version where the Evil Stepmother thinks she's eating Snow White's internal organs *didn't* make it into the Disney film. Can't think why.

For those of you who need a refresher on the plot, let's take a whistle-stop tour through its key points. Snow White is beloved by all except her wicked stepmother, the queen – a role I played in a production at the Opera House Manchester in 2019. I'll say more about this particular villainous role in the next chapter – it's probably my favourite – but suffice it to say it's the panto baddie with the least opportunity for comic asides. She's ruthless, obsessed with being the most beautiful woman in the land. So obsessed, in fact, that she has an all-seeing, all-knowing magic mirror who can answer her factually when she asks it whether she is 'the fairest of them all'. Dame Judi Dench caused quite the stir when she starred as the voice of the mirror in Theatre Royal Bury St Edmunds' production of *Snow White* in 2023 – her first appearance in pantomime, which she made to support the theatre, of which she is a life patron.

When one day the magic mirror proclaims Snow White the fairest and not her, the queen sends the huntsman (or in some versions, a pair of bumbling fools who work for her) into the forest to murder her, and to bring proof of Snow's death in the shape of her heart. You can already see why jokey asides are a bit harder to cram into this one . . .

The huntsman is so taken by Snow White that he allows her to escape, but only on condition that she never return. A poor pig or boar, depending on the version of the story, has to step in on the heart front, to trick the queen into believing the huntsman has completed his mission. Snow White flees deep into the forest, where she befriends the seven dwarfs: Happy, Sneezy, Sleepy, Dopey, Doc, Bashful and Grumpy.

In the panto version, an additional character is added as a

comedic sidekick for Snow White, a best friend called Muddles, who is the main interactor with the audience – much like Cinderella's pal, Buttons. And, like Buttons, he has an unrequited crush on his friend.

Ultimately the queen learns of her servant's failure to murder Snow White, and like many women before her she concludes that, if you want a job done, you're best off doing it yourself. She disguises herself as an old woman and heads into the forest to tempt Snow White with a poisoned apple. The apple sends Snow White into a deep sleep, and the bereft dwarfs, believing her to be dead but unwilling to bury her, place her in a glass coffin, from which she will be wakened by 'true love's kiss' when she is discovered some time later by a prince on a hunting trip. In the Brothers Grimm version, it's a considerably less romantic solution* that wakes Snow White up, as the apple is dislodged from her throat when the prince's servants stumble carrying the coffin. If only the dwarfs had known the Heimlich manoeuvre.

You can see how *Snow White*'s plot throws up issues for productions today. The prince being unable to resist kissing Snow takes on a different hue in an age where consent is not just understood but a legal necessity. And the use of CGI to portray the dwarfs in the 2025 live-action film of *Snow White* was supposed to be a way to avoid grotesque stereotypes and ableism, but it ended up backfiring. Some actors with dwarfism felt excluded from the opportunity the roles created, while comedian and author Fats Timbo felt it othered them, describing the use of CGI as treating little people as 'mythical creatures'.[2]

* Although arguably the notion of being woken by a kiss *was* the Brothers Grimm's idea, appearing in their 'Little Briar Rose' tale.

Increasingly the 'and the Seven Dwarfs' bit of the Walt Disney film's title (which was not in the title of the Brothers Grimm fairy tale) is being dropped in new panto productions.

Sometimes children play the dwarfs in the pantomime, though this can create havoc, just because children are less predictable than adults. We had children – or 'babes' as they were called then – playing the dwarf roles in the earlier productions of *Snow White* that I performed in. The kids were aged roughly between eight and ten and wore rubber heads to look like each of the seven dwarfs, and they danced like puppets on strings. More recent productions of *Snow White* that I've been in have taken their lead from *Spamalot*, in which the knights were played by adults on their knees. It must be agony on the knees – you couldn't pay me to do it!

It's to be expected that centuries-old tales will need to be updated to meet the mores of the times they're being performed in. And *Snow White* is far from the only one to be revised and tweaked to feel more suited to the moment. Another is . . .

## *SLEEPING BEAUTY*

Unsurprisingly, the origin of this panto favourite was yes, you guessed it, a fairy tale – and the inevitable Disney film of course heavily influenced the look and style of modern productions. The first pantomime version we know of was performed at Drury Lane in 1806, billed as 'A Grand Legendary Melodrama'.

*Sleeping Beauty* the pantomime is much the same as the version we know and love from the traditional story and 1959

Disney film. A king and queen who have long wished for a child and are finally granted that wish with a baby girl. They invite all the fairies in the land to attend her christening, but fail to invite one fairy, because she can be a bit of a downer. This fairy goes by the name Carabosse in the Charles Perrault and Brothers Grimm fairy tales, as well as in Tchaikovsky's ballet of *Sleeping Beauty*, but she is called Maleficent in the Disney film. Pantomime productions generally retain the original name of Carabosse, despite a new 2014 film starring Angelina Jolie as the titular Maleficent.

Of course, the royal parents leaving out Carabosse/Maleficent is a dangerous error, and after the fairies have bestowed gifts such as beauty and kindness on the baby girl, the uninvited fairy turns up anyway and bestows her own gift – a curse. The baby will reach her sixteenth birthday, then prick her finger on a spinning wheel's spindle and die. Not exactly a conventional christening gift. The best the other fairies can do is for one of them to reduce the baby's death sentence to a sleep of a hundred years.

In desperation, the king banishes all spinning wheels from the realm and the baby grows up to be a beautiful and kind girl of sixteen. Not to be outdone, our evil fairy sneaks a spinning wheel into the castle, disguising herself as an old crone, and the young princess duly pricks her finger on the spindle, falling instantly into a deep sleep.

Unable to bear the loss of their daughter, and to ensure Beauty will not be alone on her waking, the king and queen call on the good fairy again, to cast a spell that will put the whole palace into the same deep sleep. A hundred years pass by with the entire palace sleeping, and briars and thorns grow around the castle. A passing prince fights his way in, finds the sleeping princess and falls in love on sight. He kisses her and she wakes (along with all her family and the court), and they live happily ever after.

Some more recent pantomime productions have the prince meet Beauty at her sixteenth birthday party before she falls into her deep sleep, and show that they're mutually smitten. This serves a dual purpose. On one hand, it ensures that if a famous actor is appearing in the prince role, they don't just pop up at the very end – i.e. the audience gets to see more of the star they came for and the producers get their money's worth – but it also somewhat gets around the issue of consent since we know, at least, that Beauty is in love with the prince. In these productions, the prince has to be assisted by the good fairy to travel into the future in order to wake Beauty, otherwise she'd be faced with a pretty decrepit suitor, if he lived that long.

Another change to the pantomime version from the fairy tale and film is the added character of a best friend for Beauty. Strangely, she has the same best friend as panto Snow White: Muddles. Clearly he's in the market for fairy-tale princess besties. Like Snow White's Muddles, his role here is to provide some light relief, as well as acting as interlocutor with the audience.

I'll be appearing in *Sleeping Beauty* for the first time in 2026 – and you won't be surprised by which role I'm playing . . .

## *JACK AND THE BEANSTALK*

A close second favourite to *Cinderella* in terms of the number of performances in recent years, *Jack and the Beanstalk* is unusual in being one of the few beloved panto stories not to have been made into a major Disney film.

There is a *Mickey and the Beanstalk* short film, which makes up part of a 1947 compilation film called *Fun and Fancy Free*, and there was a silent version back in 1922. An animated musical version called *Gigantic* was shelved in 2017, so at the time of writing, there has still been no feature-length Disney adaptation.

It's also unusual in that it wasn't one of the fairy tales popularised by the Brothers Grimm. Research published in 2016 claims the story has its roots in a Proto-Indo-European story, 'The Boy Who Stole the Ogre's Treasure'. The first printed version that we know of was published by Joseph Roberts in a 1734 collection, where it was called 'The Story of Jack Spriggins and the Enchanted Bean'. The version that we see in panto today, however, leans more heavily on the one published by Benjamin Tabart in 1807, which adds a morality lesson at the end of the story. It goes something like this . . .

Jack and his mother live in poverty, and in desperation she sends him to market to sell their last cow. Instead, he trades the cow for beans from a mysterious stranger on the road. Infuriated, his mother throws the beans on the ground, and the eponymous beanstalk springs up overnight. Jack climbs the stalk, higher and higher, till he comes to a kingdom in the sky. Reaching a giant's house, he meets the giant's wife, who gives him food, but urges him to hide when her husband returns, in case he sniffs Jack out.*

Jack sneaks away, stealing a bag of gold as he goes. He cannot resist climbing back up the beanstalk again and again, stealing a

* Intriguingly, the giant's trademark line, 'Fee-fi-fo-fum, I smell the blood of an Englishman', is taken from Shakespeare's *King Lear*: 'Fie, foh, and fum, I smell the blood of a British man'.

golden goose which lays golden eggs, then a golden harp, which cries out to its master that it is being stolen. The giant chases Jack down the beanstalk, but Jack's mother brings him an axe just in time, and he fells the beanstalk, causing the giant to plummet to his death. In Tabart's version, Jack is given a justification for thieving from and ultimately killing the giant because he learns that the giant killed his father. And once the giant is slain, he and his mother vow to live a quiet life from then on, having learned the lesson that greed is bad. Earlier versions omitted the finger-wagging element, as do most pantos of *Jack and the Beanstalk*, which tend to end in celebrations at the defeat of the giant.

Jack also has a famous incarnation in musical theatre, as one of the fairy-tale characters in Stephen Sondheim's *Into the Woods.* In this production Jack's actions in cutting down the beanstalk and killing the giant lead to the terrible revenge of the giant's wife on the entire county and a hefty debate on the concept of consequences.

Despite there being no major Disney adaptation of the fairy tale, the pantomime version is happily flourishing and keeping the story alive, along with children's books. This was the very first pantomime I ever appeared in, as I mentioned in the Introduction – and the only one I've performed in in Australia. I played a character that is unique to the panto version, called Freddy Fleshcreep. More than the giant, he is the main villain in the pantomime, and he is designed, as his name suggests, to make the flesh creep. He's a sycophantic henchman of the giant, tricking our hero into climbing the beanstalk and committing all sorts of felonious acts. The impracticality of having to depict a giant on stage is probably why this character was brought in.

I went to see *Jack and the Beanstalk* at the Palladium one year and loved it. It was so brilliantly done, with the tree growing from the bean in front of our eyes, all the way up to the ceiling, and Jack climbing it to the top. You won't catch me shimmying up a tree, however much I love panto! I remember thinking, 'Wow, they must have spent millions on this.' It really was a spectacular version of this old classic.

## *ALADDIN*

*Aladdin* is another of the pantos that have undergone some updating to bring them in line with modern sensibilities. The story is associated with *One Thousand and One Nights*, a collection of folk tales initially compiled during the Islamic Golden Age (roughly between the eighth and fourteenth centuries), which drew from countries as diverse as Persia (modern-day Iran), India, Syria and Egypt, and reached European audiences in the eighteenth century thanks to various translations. But it wasn't part of the original Arabic text, and makes its first appearance in a French translation of 1704–14 by Antoine Galland, who heard it from a Syrian storyteller named Hanna Diyab.

This earliest pantomime iteration of *Aladdin* is set in China. For a long time, productions kept the Chinese setting, and as Neil Hurst, who played Buttons with me in 2025, reflected, they usually featured deeply problematic 'yellowface': 'When I first started, actors were still drawing lines on their eyes in an effort to make us look what would have been called "Oriental" at the time. Unimaginable now, thankfully.'

Regardless of the changing locations, the story is roughly consistent: it's your classic rags-to-riches tale. Aladdin is a poor but good-natured boy, who lives with his widowed mother in the city and develops a crush on the princess of the realm. The princess is tired of her privileged but controlled existence and is desperate to see the real world.

Aladdin falls prey to an evil trickster/sorcerer, who shows him gardens of beautiful riches, before employing him to go into the Cave of Wonders to retrieve a lamp. Once inside, the sorcerer collapses the cave in on Aladdin, demanding he hand the lamp over to him. Aladdin refuses and is trapped inside, where he rubs the lamp (or a magical ring, in some versions) without thinking. A genie appears, offering to grant him whatever he wishes. Aladdin, determined to woo the princess, asks the genie to make him a prince with untold wealth – and lo, that's what he gets, as well as the princess's heart.

But the sorcerer is still on his trail, and tricks the princess into giving him the lamp, pretending to be a salesman offering to exchange 'old lamps for new'. Aladdin must overcome the sorcerer's schemes to steal the lamp back, as well as confessing his true nature to the princess. Using his wits and the genie's power, Aladdin must defeat the sorcerer and win his now wife's love anew, proving that he is worth more than his wealth.

Today's pantomimes tend to follow the lead of later iterations of the story, and indeed the Disney versions, in locating it in an unspecified Arabic nation – leading to plenty of no less problematic productions than the China-situated version. Many pantomime performances that came after the 1992 Disney animated feature used the now famous song 'A Whole New World' and featured a princess of the same name as the film, Jasmine. As times move on, this version is understandably increasingly criticised for its lazy stereotypes of Arabic culture and people.

The tale's complicated and varied origins make it astonishing that it has survived at all, never mind thrived as one of the most popular stories on our panto stages today. Like *Cinderella*, I guess it feeds our eternal desire for the belief that a split second could change our fortunes for the better.

## *PETER PAN*

And now we come to the last of the major pantomime tales that dominate our stages today – one that I've been in a few times as that glitteringly wicked character, Hook. This is the only story used in panto that has royalties payable on it, due to author J. M. Barrie bequeathing the UK copyright to Great Ormond Street Hospital in perpetuity, which was upheld by an Act of Parliament in 1988.

*Peter Pan* used to be *the* Christmas show to see, running for years in London at the Scala and the Coliseum. Like most of the popular pantomime stories, the version we know today is an amalgamation. While we tend to think of it first appearing as Barrie's 1911 novel *Peter and Wendy*, he originally wrote it as a stage play, *Peter Pan; or, The Boy Who Wouldn't Grow Up* (1904). It was only following the play's popularity that he worked it into the longer-form book. Then, of course, like so many of these tales, it found its way onto the big screen thanks to Walt Disney, whose 1953 vision largely dictates how we imagine Peter Pan today.

The story goes more or less like this in each version: Peter Pan refuses to grow up and so lives in Neverland with his best friend, the fairy Tinker Bell, and his gang of Lost Boys. While Peter is exploring the Darling family's home in London (some pantomime productions change the location to whichever town it's being put on in), he is disturbed and in his rush to escape, the window is closed on him, severing his shadow from his body. When he goes to recover it, he meets Wendy and her brothers, John and Michael, who he teaches to fly and persuades to join him in Neverland. Once there, they meet the Lost Boys, and have magical adventures, encountering mermaids and pirates.

That's where my role comes in: Hook, the captain of the pirates. I've sometimes leaned into a *Pirates of the Caribbean* Jack Sparrow-style drunk version of him, and at other times I've played him as more menacing – having him lust after the mermaids, but because he wants to eat them, not sleep with them, using his hook to fish them out of the water. He's a gift of a character, really: driven by his desire for revenge on Peter Pan for feeding his hand to a crocodile, of which he now has a deep abiding terror, he is a wonderful mix of intelligent and foolish, debonair and charming, yet cruel and mean.

As a way of getting to his nemesis, Hook captures Wendy, John and Michael, so Peter and the Lost Boys must go to their rescue. An epic battle takes place on Hook's pirate ship, but finally Peter manages to force Captain Hook overboard, where a ticking crocodile (who'd accidentally swallowed a clock) is waiting for him. In the panto version, Hook attempts to swim away in a panic, either swimming off stage pursued by the crocodile, or being eaten by it, and the Lost Boys declare victory.

Tinker Bell sprinkles the pirate ship with fairy dust, and they fly it home to the Darlings' house. Wendy, John and Michael bid a sorrowful farewell to Peter, who cannot stay in their world, as he is the boy who never grows up.

There is something so poignant about this story – about the pure joy of being a child, and the wild imaginations we lose when we grow up; about potential lost and the paths not taken . . . It plays to each audience member in different ways: the kids are fully swept up in the magic of the story, and the flying and Peter and the Lost Boys taking on the evil pirate Hook and winning; the older audience members can understand and feel Wendy's sorrow at knowing that it's time to grow up and leave the world of Neverland behind. Stage and screen legend Bonnie Langford, who has played the title role in *Peter Pan* several times over the years, identifies an important lesson at the heart of it:

*There's a scene that's instrumental in most pantomimes and if it's not there, I get quite upset about it, as I think it's really important to teach young people that you can lose something and things will still turn out all right. In* Cinderella *it's when the Ugly Sisters come in and say, 'You can't go to the ball,' and they rip Cinderella's ticket up – or sometimes they make her rip it up herself, which is much crueller. In* Peter Pan, *that scene is where Tinker Bell is dying because she drank poison that was meant for Peter – that moment where a friend has stood in for you and paid the cost, and you suddenly realise you could lose the one thing you love or that means something to you. From that moment on the show is really instructional: although Tinker Bell is revived, it shows kids that you can lose something but can also gain something back that is probably more valuable in the end. It's important to have those profound moments in pantomime, otherwise there's a danger it can just reduce to lots of screaming.*

While I love that about the story, I think I like playing Hook so much because he's not really a part of the pathos of it all (ticking clock metaphor aside!) and I can go to town on his mean streak.

We're about to come to the 'stock' roles of panto in the next chapter, and like all the other stories I've talked about in this chapter, the panto version of *Peter Pan* has these roles carefully woven in. The 'fairy' is often Tinker Bell, of course, but if she is played by more of a variety performer – a dancer or an acrobat, say – who is fulfilling the 'act' element of a pantomime, then the 'fairy' role can be taken on by a mermaid or another magical creature. The comic character is Smee and the Dame is Mrs Smee. Peter Pan is still often played by the Principal Girl – one of the few male roles still played by women in panto – though he can also be played by the Principal Boy, with Wendy of course being the love interest. And Hook is the perfectly me-shaped villain.

## *MOTHER GOOSE*

Before we discuss the various roles within panto, I did want to touch on another play that has seen some exciting adaptations in recent years. One new production in particular provides a great example of how stories that could be seen as outdated can be brought back to life for a fresh audience. *Mother Goose* has gone through several iterations over the centuries, but loosely, the plot we know today is of a poor woman, Mother Goose, whose financial problems are solved by the arrival of a golden-egg-laying goose. Sadly, the one thing Mother Goose wants more than money is youth and beauty, and so she agrees to trade the goose to a demon for the promise of being granted those two qualities. As she believes she has been transformed into a younger, more attractive woman, her behaviour changes and alienates the other villagers and she loses all her friends – the lesson being that neither money nor beauty can buy you happiness. Long story short, she ultimately does the right thing and finds a way to rescue the goose.

Vikki Stone and Tonderai Munyevu co-wrote a reimagining of *Mother Goose*, called *Mama Goose* – featuring music by Robert Hyman – for the Theatre Royal Stratford East, which ran from November 2025 to January 2026. *Mother Goose* is one of the more old-fashioned pantomimes, so it was a surprising choice for a contemporary take. Vikki explains their reasoning:

Mother Goose *is the only pantomime that centres the Dame as the protagonist, and it was a title neither Tonderai Munyevu nor I had worked on before. We had a clear vision: to create a bold, no-nonsense African Dame as our titular Mama, surrounded by a cohort of ridiculous characters, including AI female love interest created by a character called Bougie Fierce Fairy. Because it's one of the few pantomimes not based on a fairy tale (and it hasn't been Disneyfied), we felt we could really push the boundaries of where the story could take us.*

I love that Vikki and Tonderai were not put off by what could be seen by some as a rather trad story, and that the lack of a Disney adaptation appealed to them as giving them more creative licence. I hope that their ingenuity inspires more new writers to come into the world of pantomime and see what a wealth of material there is to play with.

Ultimately, it's not hard to see why all of these stories have remained so popular with audiences when performed on the pantomime stage. They inject fantasy and escapism into our lives, while exploring themes that are all too real for many of the people going to watch them: financial hard times, unrequited love, family fallings out . . . And each has that all-important baddie to yell at and air our frustrations on. For two hours we get to live out our fantasies of a better life, of the villains getting their comeuppance, and of all the messy threads of our lives being tied up in a neat bow. If only reality could be quite so simple.

GUEST STAR

# SIMON CALLOW CBE

What to say about this next guest appearance? Simon Callow is a legendary actor, known both for his classical stage performances and for starring in films including *Four Weddings and a Funeral* and *A Room with a View*. He is also an erudite writer, both of his own memoirs and of biographies of Orson Welles and Wagner, among others, a theatre director, a musician and, yes, a panto star. His knowledge of and respect and love for the genre run deep, and he has been a vocal supporter of it for many years. In 2005, he starred as Abanazar in *Aladdin* at the Richmond Theatre.

*You've written beautifully about falling in love with pantomime as a child. I was introduced to it when I was a little older, in my late teens/early twenties, and it took considerably longer to become as enraptured as I am with it now. Do you think watching pantomimes as a child is the key to avoiding snobbery/wariness towards it?*

Well, it can't but help, can it? But it's true that when you enter a panto auditorium, you have to suspend a lot of your adult expectations. You have to be prepared to be amused, outraged, enchanted, carried away. You really do have to participate. This is not a passive art form. But this is how theatre always was until the high Victorians decided that theatres were temples of art. This is how they were in the ancient Greek theatre and in the Middle Ages and in the Elizabethan theatre. In Georgian England, the audience was pretty well out of control, and the great artists were the ones who could manage them (for a bit). Panto throws us right back to the ancient carnival tradition.

*What would you say is the greatest misconception about pantomime?*

That it's one thing – it's not: it's a lot of things, sometimes going on simultaneously. Just as many of the smuttier jokes go above the kiddies' heads.

*Did you find it useful to draw on your classical training when doing pantomime, since there are many parallels between, for example, Shakespeare's plays and pantomime?*

Well, you certainly need a lot of voice – of vocal authority, perhaps I should say – and the great classical roles simply can't be done without that. On the other hand, Shakespeare and the great classics generally are about profound psychological exploration and even its biggest fan wouldn't accuse panto of that.

*Audience participation is non-negotiable in panto. Do you enjoy it, and have you had any tricky audience situations you had to work around?*

I adore it. It can easily get out of hand, though. You have to guard against any one section of the audience letting the relaxed nature of the genre go to their heads – we love witty backchat from the audience, but if it disrupts the rest of the audience's enjoyment it has to be nipped in the bud. Which is sometimes quite hard to do.

*Do you prefer to watch pantomime or perform in it? I love both, but for different reasons, so am curious to hear from someone else who's been on both sides!*

I think I've gone beyond the age where I can cope with twelve performances a week at full tilt, vocally and physically. So I think it's a seat in the stalls for me.

*Is there a role in pantomime you haven't played that you'd like to – and if so, which and why?*

The only role I've played in panto is Abanazar, and I've done that twice. Despite what I've just said above, if I was asked again, I'd probably find it hard to resist.

*What are some of the pitfalls for pantomime as an actor, particularly one coming to it for the first time?*

It's very easy to think that it's just a lark and to get high on the audience's responses. Actually, you need iron discipline, or they start to feel excluded. If the actors start enjoying themselves too much, the audience ceases to do so.

*Do you have a favourite pantomime, either to watch or to perform in?*

Guess what? I think *Aladdin* is pretty well perfect in its combination of sex, comedy, peril, suspense and sheer madness. I haven't mentioned the only other panto I've done, because I think it isn't one – *Peter Pan*, which is a play, and needs psychological realism to make it work. The panto audience doesn't want that. It wants a madcap fantasy war between good and evil with preposterous and outrageous characters and inherently hilarious characters – clowns, in fact. *Peter Pan* can provide none of that. It's a psychological drama written by a very odd man who had an obsession about the loss of youth. You have to squeeze out the laughs with all sorts of extraneous routines. No, *Aladdin*'s the one for me, though I have a residual affection for my very first panto, *Puss in Boots*, starring Jimmy Edwards at the Streatham Hill Theatre, in 1958: a mad caper which made me fall in love with it for ever.

# 3

# WHO'S WHO?

## THE KEY ROLES OF PANTOMIME

It won't surprise you to learn that I've always played the villain in the pantomime productions I've been in. I'm known for being the 'nasty one' on *Strictly*, so it wouldn't make sense for people to come to see me play a nice guy. Personally, I think it's by far the most fun part to play in any panto, but each character has a crucial function, and who better to offer up insights into those roles than the performers who play them each year.

There is a whole set of core roles that appear across pantomimes – they'll all have individual character names in each of the shows, but their job within the plot is pretty much the same each time:

### PRINCIPAL GIRL AND PRINCIPAL BOY

These are the hero and heroine of the show, and the 'good' ones. E.g. Cinderella and the prince (*Cinderella*), Snow White and the prince (*Snow White*), Aladdin and the princess (*Aladdin*).

### DAME

This is a comedic character who interacts with the audience. E.g. Widow Twankey (*Aladdin*), Dame Trott (*Jack and the Beanstalk*) and the titular Mother Goose. The Ugly Sisters (*Cinderella*) serve a dual purpose, being 'Dame' roles as well as a comedy duo (see below).

### SIDEKICK

Like the Dame, this role is there to interact with the audience, particularly the children. E.g. Buttons (*Cinderella*),

Muddles (*Snow White*, *Sleeping Beauty*) and 'Silly Billy' (who used to be known as 'Simple Simon', but to avoid offence this was changed in recent years) in *Jack and the Beanstalk*.

### COMEDY DUO

Unlike the 'sidekick', these are bad guys, usually servants of the main villain. Aside from the Ugly Sisters, comedy duos include the henchmen (*Snow White*) and Silly Simon and Daft Dave (*Jack and the Beanstalk*).

### VILLAIN

This role is self-explanatory, really! The villain is the wicked nemesis of our hero/heroine. E.g. the Evil Stepmother or Baroness Hardup (*Cinderella*); the Evil Queen/Stepmother (*Snow White*); Hook (*Peter Pan*), etc.

### FAIRY (OR SOME OTHER MYSTICAL/MAGICAL CHARACTER)

This is a magical creature who helps intervene when all seems lost, e.g. the Fairy Godmother in *Cinderella*. It doesn't have to be an actual fairy – in *Peter Pan*, for example, it could be a mermaid performing the same function. There is usually at least one fairy in *Jack and the Beanstalk*, acting as a helpful guide to Jack and a foil to the giant's evil henchman, Freddy Fleshcreep. The fairy is one 'stock' character that doesn't always appear in pantos – there isn't a specific 'fairy' or 'magic' character in *Snow White*, for example.

Pantomime's Italian ancestor, *Commedia dell'arte*, and some of its main characters: Harlequin, Columbine, Pantaloon and the clown.

The Romans celebrated the festival Saturnalia in December – with lots of role reversal, naughty behaviour and generalised chaos. Its influence on panto is clear!

WRalston

The Day of Misrule was popular in medieval and Tudor England: a 'king' was appointed from the lower classes to oversee twelve days of revelry.

This, and the plays of Shakespeare, which appealed to a broad demographic, working on many different levels, had a clear role to play in shaping pantomime.

While 'mummers' wore masks, mumming had much in common with panto, whether the very tailored, localised performances they put on, the mix of humour, singing and dancing in the shows, or the festive timing.

John Rich (1682–1761), often heralded as the 'father of pantomime', playing the Harlequin, a role he became fêted for.

Let's head backstage to find out a bit more about each of these roles, and to hear from the actors who play them about their understanding of these panto parts – and their experiences performing them.

## PRINCIPAL GIRL AND PRINCIPAL BOY

As the word 'Principal' suggests, these roles are the main ones: they *are* the story, and everyone else's job is to help facilitate their storyline. In the past, the Principal Boy was played by a woman, but increasingly these days, men will play this role – if any Principal Boy role is still played by a woman these days, it's usually that of Peter in *Peter Pan*, as we saw in the previous chapter. The Principal Girl role is played by a woman.

As well as being the main characters, the key thing about the Principal Boy and Girl is that they are inherently good. They find themselves surrounded by evil characters who try to stop them succeeding, or who try to corrupt them, or get something from them. Their role is either to convert evil to good, or to destroy evil. In that way, pantomimes are like morality tales: good always triumphs. When it comes to the actors playing these roles, Principal Boys are stereotypically tall and handsome and Principal Girls are beautiful: they have to be like Disney princes and princesses, essentially. They have to look true to the archetype of that character – and to be able to belt out pop love songs these days, of course!

Elly Jay played the titular heroine to my Evil Stepmother in the Theatre Royal Nottingham production of *Cinderella* in December 2025. It was her fifth professional panto, though she'd performed in pantomimes since she was a kid, up in Fraserburgh, a fishing village in the northeast of Scotland. Those early experiences made her a fan of the genre: 'There's just something for everyone. I'm so happy that over the generations it has stuck as part of the culture. Of all things it brings everybody together at Christmas.' She recalls rehearsing for weeks for shows like *Dick Whittington* and *Sleeping Beauty* when she was a child, the opposite to the lightning-fast rehearsal periods we have for professional performances – a couple of weeks if we're lucky.

It's not all upside being the Principal Girl, as Elly reflects:

*Sometimes as the princess, you miss having the opportunity to be funny, to be the one with the comic lines or the person everyone's booing at; those roles where they get to break the fourth wall. As the prince or princess, you don't generally break the fourth wall, unless you introduce yourself to the audience early on. You don't have licence to do it, other than that. Sometimes, I'll ask the director, 'Oh, can I do a little joke here?' and the answer is always, 'No, you're the princess.'*

With the graciousness of the princesses she usually plays, however, Elly continues: 'I have always wanted to play Cinderella and Sleeping Beauty, though, and I've done both of them, so I'm not complaining!'

Stephenson Ardern-Sodje, who played Prince Charming in that same Nottingham show with us, says, 'I think what we get to do is tell the earnest and more sweet side of the story, which is comforting for people. For a lot of kids, panto might be their first exposure to traditional storytelling, alongside Disney. And we get to be the vessel for that.'

Those roles of Principal Boy and/or Girl really help set the framework of every pantomime. Their story has to follow its set path; it allows the audience to relax into the fairy-tale narrative they know and love, and permits the other actors around them to be able to play and improvise, knowing that central narrative is held firmly in place.

## DAME

People often assume that I've played panto Dames – presumably because I wear drag in panto – but it's a completely different role to the villain, with its own set of rules. The Dame is generally played by a man dressed as a woman, but crucially, they are not trying to look like a real woman. They're normally sort of grotesque, with over-the-top make-up and big colourful hair and eyebrows up to their hairline. Sometimes they wear prosthetics to emphasise their backsides and breasts. It's a whole schtick. As well as their physical appearance, the actors playing the Dame generally put on a high-pitched false voice; it's intended as a caricature.

I've only played opposite a Dame once, because I'm already a man in drag and there's generally a desire to avoid having two men in drag in the same show, even if one's a villain and one is a good character. A lot of the shows are quite male-heavy, so as well as not wanting to have two actors in drag drawing the attention away from one another, it's just good to make sure there's a balance in the cast. Sometimes we'll make villains like Freddy Fleshcreep a woman – Mrs Fleshcreep – if there's a male Fairy Godmother, for instance.

The Dame, of course, is on the side of good and helps the Principal Boy and Girl hold the story together. They're always the one talking to the audience, breaking the fourth wall to ask questions like 'What do you think of him? Isn't that nasty person *horrible*?', letting them know that they can vocalise their dislike of the villains.

With a man playing the Dame, there is potential for comedy moments that could really only happen if the bosoms are padded or fake – a bit like Robin Williams in the film *Mrs Doubtfire.** And if a man's wearing a big fake wig that falls off, as has happened to me in panto, that's a real laugh you'll hear from the cast as well as the audience.

As we've seen with other aspects of pantomime, as times change, so do attitudes to roles, and today as many women play the Dame as men. Ultimately, the Dame's role is to encourage the audience and teach them what they need to do throughout the show, and anyone can play that part. That said, I do hope that drag doesn't disappear from our panto stages – and not just because I happen to rock a gown myself . . . Elly Jay puts it thoughtfully:

*I do think pantomime reminds people that we need to be a lot kinder . . . That we should let people express themselves however they choose to through what they wear, or show a different version*

* Williams's character wants to appear realistic as a woman, but instead ends up a little pantomime, particularly when the fake breasts he's wearing catch fire and he uses saucepan lids to put them out.

*of themselves. All it is is literally make-up and a wig and a pair of heels. It's strange when you see people condemning drag and saying it's wrong for children to see things like* RuPaul's Drag Race. *I just think, hang on a minute, you've been watching pantomimes for years, with men dressing up as women, and you've had fun. I really do believe that there is something at the core of pantomime that is about giving us a foundation for treating each other kindly in a world that is constantly changing and evolving.*

Proper, old-fashioned Dames are a dying breed. Terry Scott, best known for the popular BBC sitcom *Terry and June* and the *Carry On* films, was a wonderful comic Dame who died in 1994. Many of the remaining classic Dame actors are getting older and it's a very physical role. In 2024, following his final performance at the Grand Opera House in York in 2023, Berwick Kaler, the longest-serving pantomime Dame, retired. He had performed the Dame role for an astonishing forty-seven years, putting my own two decades of playing the villain in the shade. Back in 2003, to mark twenty-five years in pantomime, he was granted the freedom of the city of York, and an honorary degree from the University of York. There really is nothing like a Dame.

## SIDEKICK

The sidekick is often the butt of the joke in the pantomime, but like the Dame, they're always on the side of good, so we're rooting for them. They sometimes have unrequited feelings for the Principal Girl, so there's a degree of pathos, too. Perhaps the key to this role is that it's the character in a panto that the kids in the audience can best relate to – he (it's usually a male role) likes to be silly and play games, just like them. He's typically best friends with the Principal Boy or Girl, but is not unattainably perfect like them, nor scary like the villain, nor over the top like the Dame.

This is another character that speaks directly to the audience, and it's generally their role to rally the kids and provide comedy, often in a double act with the Dame. It's usually the sidekick who opens proceedings, coming out to greet the audience, telling them his name and that every time he comes on stage they should shout 'Hello, [Buttons, Muddles, etc.]'. And they're usually the one to bring the panto to an end, with the Dame, for the 'song sheet' – the closing musical number.*

Despite occupying the place of the 'fool' – or the clown in *commedia* – the sidekick isn't a simple part to play: they have to get the audience warmed up and shouting out or booing, while keeping the interaction carefully contained to specific moments so it doesn't disrupt the main story. There's a reason this character is often played by a children's entertainer!

The brilliant Neil Hurst has appeared in thirty-one pantomimes since he was eighteen years old, and always in comic sidekick roles, including Buttons, Silly Billy and Wishy Washy. He's the perfect person to reveal more about this particular stock character of panto.

* So called because a sheet used to be displayed on stage for the audience to sing along to. Nowadays the closing song is usually so familiar that the audience will know the words.

*Initially I think I was cast in this role because I was young and energetic – it does get harder as you get older, but it never becomes any less enjoyable. I like to play the comic sidekick role as a naughty schoolboy, very much on side with the kids. When I started out, I definitely played it more safe than I do now, making more kid-friendly jokes. Nowadays I've learnt that the secret is, it's a family show, but that doesn't mean it's solely for the kids. After all, it's the grown-ups who are buying the tickets, so you have to engage them as much as you're engaging the kids. It took me a few years to realise, 'Oh, actually, I can be naughty, I can say stuff that's a little bit rude or cheeky.'*

That said, it's a fine line. 'I'm a parent myself,' he notes, 'and I sometimes think, "I wouldn't say that to my daughters so I shouldn't say that here."' The times change and so does what is deemed funny, and it's a testament to Neil's ability as a performer that he's only ever had one complaint about his jokes in his career: 'I made a joke that went something like, "Me mum's very poorly. She's got hay fever and diabetes, so I've tried to cheer her up with flowers and chocolates." I got in trouble for it because there were some diabetic kids in and their parents wanted money back. I apologised, of course.'

Interactions with the audience are fraught with risk – it's impossible to know exactly who you're speaking to as they're quite literally strangers in the crowd. You're not going to know what they personally find funny or not, or what they are comfortable with. Neil enjoys the shows that are specifically for schools because he knows who will be a safe – and welcome – target: teachers. 'I'm basically like a grandparent getting the kids all riled up and buzzing on sweeties! I tell them to shout and boo at their teachers, then send them back home. Off you go!'

He loves the anarchy of the sidekick role and its interactions with the audience. There really is a lot of art to it, and it takes a great amount of skill to master it as he has. (Jonathan Kiley, casting director at Crossroads, believes that Buttons is the most famous comedy role in pantomime because it has pathos – he loves Cinderella but never gets the girl – and making the audience laugh while also being able to make them cry takes real talent.) Now in his forties, Neil is beginning to think that he'll need to change more than just his jokes before too long. He is considering leaving the Buttons role behind, for a very valid reason:

*I'm inevitably going to get to a point where it's weird playing this guy who's in love, unrequited, with Cinderella. Thankfully, in this production, the actor playing her is thirty, so it's fine. But if Cinderella was twenty, twenty-one, I'd just look like a dirty old man. Well, I'd feel like a dirty old man. And I don't want to feel that way. Now I'm in my forties I think the inevitable switch from playing the comic to playing the Dame is just around the corner.*

Steady on now, Neil. Keep your hands off my roles . . . He makes a good point, though. It would be weird for me to play a romantic lead in pantomime aged sixty. The kids in the audience need to be able to relate to certain roles in pantomime, whether it's the comedy sidekick or the prince and the princess. And let's face it, children think anyone over thirty is ancient, because that is the same age as their mum and dad. All kids want to imagine themselves in the main roles, whether as the poor girl who ends up marrying the prince, the prince who fights through the forest to win the heart of the girl he's fallen for, or the jokester pal who helps either one of the principal players find their heart's desire, so having younger actors play those parts is crucial.

## COMEDY DUO

Like the comedy sidekick, the comedy duos in pantomimes have traditionally been played by men, but in more recent years they've also been played by women. The Ugly Sisters in *Cinderella* were always played by men in drag, but now the actors tend to be women wearing grotesque make-up. Those particular roles – the Ugly Sisters – are an interesting mix of the Dame and the comedy duo. They're slapstick, like the Dame, and have over-the-top make-up, but like most comedic duos in panto, they are also ostensibly 'bad' characters.

It's quite surprising that the roles of the Ugly Sisters still exist – they're there for us to laugh at because they're ugly. They're never going to get the prince, simply because they're unattractive. But it's OK for us to laugh at them, because they're arrogant and unkind and they think they're beautiful, even though everyone knows they're not. Maybe it's just a brutal reflection of society: if you're unattractive, you're less likely to get a man, or to get ahead. It's not really a very contemporary message, though.

Perhaps because of this, some recent productions have taken to calling them the 'Wicked Stepsisters', as with the roles played by actors Britt Lenting and May Tether in the 2025 Nottingham production of *Cinderella*, alongside my Evil Stepmother.

Historically, physical appearance was used in pantomime to denote inner personality traits, but as society has acknowledged that it's wrong to judge people based on their looks, panto has changed too, focusing on inward characteristics over outward appearances. Physical humour hasn't disappeared entirely though: the comedy duo roles often use slapstick or play up visible differences between the two actors – usually one will be tall and skinny and the other small and larger, so they're chalk and cheese.

Like a lot of 'comedic duo' roles, despite being 'bad' characters, the sisters are mainly there to be punching bags for the villain – in this instance, their mother – just as Ratfink and Weasel, the henchmen of the Evil Queen in *Snow White* (sometimes there is just one henchman, 'Herman'),, find themselves on the receiving end of her anger in place of the heroine. They're nasty characters, but also inept, and they inevitably mess up.

There was probably a moral reason for these roles at one time, warning that if you unquestioningly fall in with a bad crowd then you'll end up being a joke at best, or locked up or dead at worst: just like many comedy duos, who either actively share the villain's aims or are cowards who simply go along with their evil plans. And they do create a counterbalance to the comedic 'good' character of the sidekick as well.

## VILLAIN

And so we come to the part I play: the villain. As I've said, on *Strictly Come Dancing* I play up the 'mean' Craig act, which works well when I'm doing panto: it makes it easy for people to see me as the 'baddie' and to instantly want to boo me on stage – which they do to the point where I can't continue with my lines! I enjoy it, to be honest, and a plus side to playing the villain rather than the Dame is that I'm meant to be glamorous. When I'm playing the Evil Stepmother in *Snow White*, or the Wicked Stepmother in *Cinderella* (stepmothers get a hard rap, don't they?), it gives me the opportunity to look as beautiful as possible, because I want to be the fairest in the land or some variety of that. That said, these characters are also getting older and fooling themselves that they look as youthful or beautiful as the Principal Girl characters – which is a bit ageist, if you ask me.

All the villainous characters in pantomime are driven by something: power, money, beauty, revenge. These are things we all want, but that when taken to an extreme can destroy us. In *Cinderella*, the stepmother is married to Baron Hardup, who unsurprisingly has no money, so she is desperate to marry off her grotesque daughters to the prince, rather than her stepdaughter, Cinderella. In *Snow White*, the stepmother's driven by her obsession to be the most beautiful woman in the land, and is determined to rid herself of Snow White, who the mirror has told her will usurp her. If I'm playing Hook, he's driven by the desire to destroy Peter Pan in revenge for throwing his hand to the crocodile to eat.

My favourite villain to play is the Evil Queen in *Snow White*, but now I'm sixty I'd think twice about doing it. She has to be very thin, and I'm not sure I want to go to quite such a physical effort for a role any more! Even so, the glamour of the part is a large factor in its appeal; another is that it's the meatiest villainous character in panto. It's a challenge: you've got many costume changes, a lot of songs and a lot of dancing. As I've said before, it's three characters in one, really: 1) the Evil Queen, 2) me as the 'Nasty Judge from *Strictly*' (or whoever the celebrity character is who's playing it) and 3) the old lady who is poisoning Snow White with the apple. All three roles have to be believable. When I'm playing the old lady, Snow White has to believe that it's someone completely different to her stepmother – that it's a lovely old lady that she can plausibly trust.

That reminds me of a glorious example of a panto villain role being written with a nod to the role the actor playing it was famous for, in this case the wonderful David Suchet. He played Hook in *Peter Pan* at the Bristol Hippodrome (2023–4 season), and at the end of the show, as he was fighting Peter Pan, he stopped and explained that he wasn't really Captain Hook. There was a transition where he took his Hook costume off and revealed himself to be Poirot, the Agatha Christie detective who made him a household name.

I've never played a 'good' character in panto, and I can't for the life of me understand why. Joking apart, I hope I do add a bit of nuance to the villains I play; after all, as 'Mr Nasty' on TV, I'm seen as nasty because I tend to tell the truth, even if it isn't very pretty. I think that makes me a villain who's fun to boo, but isn't *too* terrifying for the kids.

Villains are never victorious at the end of pantomimes: Hook gets eaten by a crocodile, the Evil Queen in *Snow White* is banished, and the Wicked Stepmother in *Cinderella* goes to prison for the rest of her life. All of them lose their power, wealth, land, everything. The villain and their followers' ultimate failure teaches us as the audience a lesson about the relative unimportance and ephemerality of money and power as opposed to the essential, timeless nature of friendship, loyalty, love and respect. They're wonderful learning curves for kids, in that way, pantomimes.

## THE FAIRY

The fairy character – usually the Fairy Godmother – performs several functions in panto (though as we've seen, she doesn't appear in every single one). Most obviously, they reassure the audience when things look bad for the hero/heroine that everything will turn out right, and they use magic to help overcome seemingly insurmountable obstacles to a happy ending. And I think there's a comforting social aspect to this role, too, particularly in the case of the Fairy Godmother in *Cinderella*. Cinders is faced with a triumvirate of evil: her stepmother, who relegates her to a servant role in the household, and her stepsisters, who hate her because she's pretty and kind when they are not. Although her father is alive, Cinderella is without any family she can turn to or rely on. But when she's in need, she always has the Fairy Godmother, who shows her that she is worthy of happiness and good fortune. This teaches the kids a lesson that actually, even if you feel like you don't belong – whether that's within your family, or at school, or among a group of kids – and however hopeless it may seem, there is someone out there who believes in you and wants to help you find your way.

In current pantos, the fairy role is often given to incredible singers, as when soul songbird Beverley Knight took on the part of Fairy Godmother in *Cinderella* at the Birmingham Hippodrome in 2017. I've already mentioned Christina Bianco, the astonishingly good impressionist and singer who sang Cher and Christina Aguilera songs, among others, in our 2025 production of *Cinderella*. She recalls getting approached to appear in pantos on her arrival in the UK a few years ago because of her vocal skills:

*I have a bit of a reputation for doing impressions [Adele, Shirley Bassey and Julie Andrews are just some of those she's known for] and when I first got here, I kept being asked to perform in pantomimes as the Fairy Godmother or the genie in* Aladdin *as those roles often go to singers nowadays. I put it off for a few years as I knew I had to sort of earn my stripes as a foreigner: I wanted to live and work in the UK longer before I did pantomime so people didn't think, 'Why are they dropping this random American into a panto?!'*

Even though her talents were what made Christina a natural pick for the Fairy Godmother role, in the production of *Cinderella* we performed in together, her part was rewritten during rehearsal week. It quickly became clear she was *so* good that the script was adapted to incorporate her skills more fully.

## ANIMAL CHARACTERS

Animals don't feature in pantomime quite as heavily as they used to, so I haven't listed them as a stock character earlier in the chapter, but they're a fabulously fun part of the show when they do appear. If you ask people what animal they most associate with pantomime, they will probably say the panto horse – that usually clumsy two-person outfit with one person playing the front of the horse and the other the back, largely played for slapstick laughs. Fun fact – there's even an annual London pantomime horse race, for charity! But despite its fame, the panto horse has never really been a frequent or prominent feature of pantomime.

There are, however, a good number of animal parts in pantomime that recur every year: Daisy the Cow from *Jack and the Beanstalk*, Puss from *Puss in Boots*, Tommy the Cat in *Dick Whittington*, Priscilla the Goose in *Mother Goose* . . . And back in the Victorian and Edwardian era, there were specialist animal impersonators who played these roles. Known as 'skin artistes', because of the full-body costumes they wore, which are called 'skins' in theatre, these actors studied how animals moved and behaved in order to provide as close a representation of them as possible on the stage. It makes sense that some of the best-known of these actors were also trained gymnasts and acrobats, given the physical flexibility it takes to move like an animal. Two actors who became immensely successful in nineteenth-century pantomime due to their extraordinary ability to play animals were Charles Lauri Jr – a trained acrobat – and Fred Conquest, who came from a dynasty of theatre actors. Lauri Jr was especially known for his portrayal of cats, including Tommy in *Dick Whittington*, while Conquest mainly played geese, cats or dogs.

Today, it's mostly Daisy the Cow that people will be used

to seeing on panto stages, or Priscilla the Goose. Like the panto horse, the cow costume is for two people. With the heat of the stage lights being a lot to contend with in normal panto costume, I can't imagine what it must be like to be in a furry outfit and having to contort yourself into animal-like postures. I hope those costumes get a good airing.

It's extremely rare that real animals are brought on stage these days – usually this would be a pony for Cinderella. However, due to animal welfare concerns, what with the bright lights and loud noises on stage, some theatres and production companies have banned the use of live animals.

There is of course one other crucial role in every pantomime that I didn't mention at the start of this chapter . . .

## THE AUDIENCE

The reason any pantomime works is the audience. They have to play a role in proceedings, and they are, just as much as those of us up on stage, a character. A mostly reliable one, but not always! It's why I don't think pantomime can ever truly work on TV or film, though there have been quite a few attempts (during Covid, a celebrity-filled production of *Cinderella* was aired on BBC Two for Comic Relief, with Olivia Colman, Anya Taylor-Joy and Helena Bonham Carter among those starring). Pantomime actors are constantly feeding off the audience's responses, so I can't imagine how hard it would be to do a filmed version. It would be like having canned laughter on sitcoms. The crew might laugh, but they're busy working, so they're not going

David Garrick. Despite being a bit snooty about pantomime, he couldn't deny its commercial potential, so staged it at the Drury Lane Theatre to great success.

The lavish 700-seater Canterbury Music Hall in Lambeth was one of the first ever purpose-built music halls. These gorgeous buildings became logical homes for staging pantomime after music hall theatre fell out of fashion.

Vesta Tilley, star of music hall theatre, was one of the first women to play 'Principal Boy' roles in pantomime, to huge acclaim.

A 'skin' is someone who specialises in playing animal roles – here's Freda Wyn, playing Boots in *Puss in Boots* back in 1957. You won't catch me doing handstands these days!

For anyone snobbish about panto – royalty performed in it! Princess Margaret and Princess Elizabeth (as she was then) here performing in *Cinderella* for the Royal Christmas pantomime at Windsor Castle in 1941.

A young Julie Andrews, by the caravan she lived in while performing in a pantomime of *Little Red Riding Hood* in 1950.

The one and only Cilla Black, who was performing in *Aladdin* at the Palladium, having a laugh as she tries her costume on for the first time.

to have the same response as an audience that's paid to come and watch you and have a night of entertainment.

The whole dynamic in pantomime is that the audience is in cahoots with the good guys. They're given the rules of interaction at the start of the show, although I sometimes think that Brits come out of the womb knowing what and when they're supposed to shout at pantos.

I honestly don't think I've ever had an unresponsive pantomime audience. There is definitely a difference in terms of volume in different regions, though. I'd say it's the case that the further north you go, the louder the reaction! Liverpool and Manchester are always raucous fun, and Scottish cities even more so. It takes a bit more to get a reaction in the South. But wherever you are in the country, people come to the shows to have fun, and because they want to be there. Yes, there are different audiences at every performance, and some might be quieter than others, but they're always enthusiastic. You do sometimes find that in the evenings, particularly on a Friday or Saturday night, adults in the audience might be more, shall we say, lubricated, and they can be extremely loud. Then you've got the hecklers, but we're giving them licence to shout and scream and react, so as long as it's all in good spirits – which it always has been, in my experience – it's part of the fun.

Generally, it gets wilder as we get closer to Christmas. People have time off work, and they've been drinking before they come in so they're already having a good time. Everyone's up for a holiday party and those are usually fantastic audiences, where they're just whooping, hollering, loving it, shouting out stuff, heckling, and I really like that. These are the people who are paying our wages, so I want them to have the best possible time. And not only that: people need an escape when times are hard. Daily life can be so tough, especially at Christmas time when there are bills to pay and taxes looming, and you've got a family to feed and might be figuring out how you're going to get through to January. And if going to a panto can relieve you of even an iota of that for a short time, then our job is done.

I see part of my role as encouraging audiences to boo me louder than they already are. At the very start of my panto career, I didn't quite know how to handle the boos, but Jonathan Kiley helpfully gave me some lines to use in those moments. I started to write them down and put them on my mirror before I went on stage, so I had things ready to say. Then the more pantos I performed in, the more I enjoyed making up my own responses. Nowadays, I genuinely think there's nothing more disappointing than a half-hearted boo. I tell the audience how pathetic they are if it's not overwhelmingly loud: 'That's the worst booing I've ever heard in my life!' So then they really go for it, and I say, 'Thank you very much, that was lovely.'

We usually get audience members up on stage at some point during pantomime productions, often during the 'song sheet', which I mentioned earlier. Although it's usually a singalong, the 'song sheet' doesn't always have to be music. Sometimes it can be a silly thing like kids being brought on stage to throw pie in the face of a comedy character. For a lot of kids, going to pantomime might be the first time they go to a theatre, so imagine then being asked to get involved like that. Thankfully, they do seem to enjoy it – the Buttons/Muddles character is, as I've said before, usually played by a children's entertainer who knows how to ensure they are having fun and don't get stressed.

Nowadays, of course, parents have to sign off authorisation for the children to go up on stage, but that doesn't ensure a kid isn't going to get upset. If they do have a bit of a wobble, it's the actor playing the comedic sidekick's role to take the focus off the kid by saying things like, 'Did that nasty Evil Queen do something to upset you? Come on everyone, let's boo the mean queen.' There are all sorts of tricks of the trade for handling these moments, and it's all part of the job. Not mine though, thankfully! Sometimes we'll use a ventriloquist, who'll put words in the kids' mouths so they don't actually have to speak, which can be played nicely for laughs too. The kids being brought on stage is a chance for them to gain in confidence: they can go home and say, 'I was on stage and I was acting with all the actors.' They're part of it.

Actor Stephenson Ardern-Sodje, whose run in the 2025–6 season of *Cinderella* at the Theatre Royal Nottingham alongside me was his first experience of acting in pantomime, admits that the younger members of the audience were one of the things he found intimidating about the form: 'Children are very honest audiences: they really do switch off if they aren't interested. If you're trying to tell a joke and it doesn't land, they let you know about it.'

There's usually one week in the middle of the season where you have schools bringing classes to watch and the kids just scream the entire time, because they're with their teachers and they're *allowed* to be unruly for once. Normally everyone's being told to shut up, but now suddenly they're being encouraged to shout. And trust me, they do. On the days we have schools in, I tend to rattle through the adult stuff so the show will become faster – I can't get the same reaction as I'll get in the evening or during other weeks, so sometimes I cut chunks of dialogue out. They're not really interested in the dialogue at all; in fact they really don't care too much about the story, but they *love* to interact with the actors and shout as much as they can. When they're meant to boo, they'll go on for minutes at a time, which as the villain is exactly the sort of response you're wanting to evoke.

Usually, when we're performing, we're conscious of the difference between the children and adults in terms of their response to us on stage. As Neil Hurst says:

*It's about understanding that it's a balance between storytelling and anarchy. If you have too much story, the kids lose interest. The kids are always waiting for anarchy and comedy. But equally, if you have too much of that, they get too agitated to enjoy the story. So you have to be flexible; sometimes I take out jokes if I think we're in danger of losing focus on the plot.*

If the comic characters are tasked with managing the younger members of the audience, it's usually more my role to deal with people who've had a bit too much to drink at the interval, although drunk adults aren't really that dissimilar to the kids. That's where playing a villain can come in handy. The Principal Boy and Girl can't break the fourth wall mid-play, but the villain absolutely can turn around and say, 'Oi, you, sit down!' I can't lie, I enjoy that part. Regardless of what the rowdier audience members do, it's our job to be equipped as a performer to handle it, to have ways of chatting back to them, while also calming them down. There's always going to be one. If they're being particularly annoying, you can always pull them out, make them stand up and sing a song. That usually shuts them up! Of course, there are times when audience members can be completely unruly or unable to control how they're behaving. The actors playing comic characters are great at responding to heckles or over-boisterous audience members, since they're often comedians who are pros at dealing with that sort of interaction. They have years' worth of material with which to handle it. The key to being a panto performer is the ability to power through regardless, and try to take the rest of the audience on a journey.

That's pretty much a roll-call of the core characters that crop up again and again across different pantomimes and the function that they play within them. There is nothing arbitrary about any of the roles; they all serve a purpose, including those I haven't gone into here. There are many more performers up on stage than appear in these roles I've just outlined – chorus parts for villagers and other supporting parts, all of which are an essential aspect of the whole. And when it comes to significant people involved in pantomime, there are even more offstage than on it. In the world of pantomime, it truly does take a village.

GUEST STAR

# LESLEY JOSEPH

A true legend of stage and screen, Lesley Joseph is owed a huge debt of gratitude by the world of pantomime. She's been a dedicated star turn in panto for decades now, putting in performances of characters across the spectrum from good to evil – from the Fairy Godmother in *Dick Whittington* and *Cinderella*, to the Wicked Queen in *Snow White and the Seven Dwarfs* – always with her trademark charm and mischief.

She is, of course, best known for her portrayal of the snobbish and lascivious character Dorien Green in beloved British sitcom *Birds of a Feather*, which ran from 1989 to 1998 and again from 2014 to 2020. Her ability to deliver more than a few double entendres over the show's duration stood her in good stead for treading the boards in panto. In 2016, she appeared in *Strictly Come Dancing*, and we also crossed paths when we shared the role of the wicked Miss Hannigan in a touring production of *Annie*, so it was fabulous to be reunited with her to discuss her time in panto.

*You're one of the few people I've spoken to for this book who's been in panto longer than I have. What keeps you coming back for more?*

I have! I've been doing it for forty years. I've got twenty years on you, darling. I love panto as it combines drama, comedy, dance, songs and almost stand-up, too, which is great for me as I love all of those things.

*And what was it that got you into pantomime in the first place?*

I got into panto with theatre producer Paul Elliott in 1991, playing the Wicked Stepmother in *Cinderella*. Paul sadly died this year, having written and directed around five hundred pantomimes, on top of producing. I had done one panto before at the Birmingham Rep, but this was very different. It was at Richmond Theatre with Michaela Strachan and Geoffrey Davies and after *Birds of a Feather* had become a hit for the BBC.

*Unlike me, you've played the 'good' characters, as well as villains – particularly a few Fairy Godmothers. Do you have a preference for playing the wicked or the good characters, and if so, why?*

Oh, I definitely prefer the villains, because you can make jokes and just inject more humour into the role generally. It's fun seeing the audience want to boo you, because you're the baddie, but then witness them being torn, because they like you as an actor, so they're still rooting for you even though you're playing the villain. When I play the 'good' roles, like the Fairy Godmother, I try to bring in some flaws to their character, or it can be a bit dull.

*You've performed in most of the major pantomimes (apart from* Mother Goose, *I think) – do you have a favourite story to perform in?*

I love *Snow White*, probably because I get to play a character in the Wicked Queen who is evil, but who has a lot of comedy added into her lines. I never want to play any character that's one-note.

*You won Panto Icon at the 2026 Pantomime Awards – congratulations! Do you have your own panto icon, perhaps someone you looked up to when you first went into it?*

Thanks, darling! They're all heroes, to me – but perhaps Paul Elliott was, in particular.

*Pantomime definitely gets looked down on by the rest of the theatre industry (and by many people in the wider world). Have you had to deal with that sort of elitism when talking about panto?*

Yes, definitely. When I started out, it was really looked down on. It was always a case of people saying, 'Have you not got any other work?' if you were doing panto. Thankfully, I think that attitudes have changed towards panto in the time that I've been performing in it and there is a lot more respect for it as a genre today – and for those of us doing it.

*In the time you've been doing panto, what do you think have been the biggest changes?*

Well, there are certain things you can't say any more! Some venues, for example, prefer you not to say 'ladies and gentlemen, girls and boys', and when you've done that for years and years, it becomes a habit, so it can be easy to forget and slip up.

But I don't think there are any changes that have been made to panto that have been for the worse, or any that would make me stop wanting to do it.

*What would your words of wisdom be for any actor venturing into panto for the first time?*

To any actor entering panto for the first time, I would just say: take it seriously and enjoy every moment. Play off the audience and put your heart and soul into every performance. Enjoy being a part of this wonderful experience.

# 4

# NO BUSINESS LIKE SHOW BUSINESS

## THE PROFESSIONAL EVOLUTION OF PANTOMIME

One of the criticisms of panto that I've heard over the years is that it can be a bit 'am dram'. 'Am dram' is a very British phrase – and the way it's become used as a putdown is even more British . . . When you think about it, 'amateur dramatics' just means non-professional stage productions: usually local performances put on for fun; for the love of it. And there are a lot of amateur panto productions staged every year across the UK – from schools to local theatre companies.

But if someone accuses something of being 'a bit am dram', they are usually making a dig at it being a bit shoddy, production-wise, and hammy in the acting department. While this might have been a legitimate accusation against many productions – even the larger-scale ones – twenty or thirty years ago, it's plainly inaccurate to level it at the professional world of panto today.

Nowadays, pantomime is big business. It's always been an important source of revenue for those working within the industry – two months of guaranteed work is never to be sniffed at. But over the time that I've been performing in it, I've seen panto become an increasingly professional outfit; from the standard of the actors' performances to the exceptionally high-quality production values of the shows, and the formidable marketing campaigns that help drive audiences through the theatre doors, it's moved into a different league.

The 2025–6 pantomime season saw approximately 260 pantomimes being put on across the country.[1] It's a huge money-spinner for theatres, often helping to keep venues afloat for the rest of the year with the revenue it brings in across the Christmas period. For anyone who looks down their nose at the genre, it's worth pointing out that it brings in £60 million to the UK economy. Little wonder that, of all forms of entertainment, PricewaterhouseCoopers, one of the Big Four accounting firms, have an annual pantomime as part of their community outreach programme.

According to industry publication *Spotlight*, pantomime 'contributes up to 50% of a UK theatre's annual revenue'.[2] The CEO and artistic director of Worcester Theatres, Sarah-Jane Morgan, has said that without panto the theatre world would struggle: 'We would see a lot more doors closing on venues and it would take the heart out of a lot of local communities as well.'[3]

It makes sense that theatres block out the Christmas months to put these productions on as reliable seat-fillers. There's also a long-term benefit: with pantomimes drawing in families with young children, a whole new generation is being shown the joys of theatre, and given a first taste of a world they will want to return to again and again.

It would be an understatement to say that panto has come a long way since its more hammy days from the 1970s through to the 1990s. While it was still popular then, it felt like a genre inching dangerously close to extinction, with faded celebrities playing out the sunset of their careers slapping their thighs and grinning at painfully old-hat jokes. As Jonathan Kiley explains:

*There was a stage in pantomime where the productions were lacklustre. The stars who were being cast just weren't very good – they were chosen solely because they were 'off the telly' – there for being famous, without having any particular acting or singing talent. We soon realised that if the public doesn't have a great*

The glorious Sir David Suchet, giving me a run for my money as Hook.

My pal Paul Chuckle winning over the crowd as the hapless henchman Oddjob in *Snow White and the Seven Dwarfs*, alongside the wonderful Lesley Joseph as the Wicked Queen – with Aaron James as Muddles sandwiched between them.

The magic touch of Pete Firman: another fabulous comic with the audience eating out of his hand as Silly Billy in *Beauty and the Beast*.

The legendary Bonnie Langford as Cinderella, here in the arms of Paul Nicholas as Buttons.

Booo, hisssss!
Simon Callow CBE,
scaring the audience
silly with his deliciously
villainous Abanazar
in *Aladdin*.

The incredible spectacle that is the London Palladium pantomime, with its dazzling sets, lighting and costumes.

The inimitable Clive Rowe MBE, who has made the role of Dame all his own, thanks to his legendary appearances at London's Hackney Empire Theatre.

*time, they don't come back, so you need people who can really deliver. Sound on stage in the old days wasn't great, either; now it's recording-level quality, and the lighting is phenomenal, too. The shows' running time was far too long back then – they used to go on forever – and it's not true that you can't have enough of a good thing. You absolutely can. Less is more; simple is best.*

The time Jonathan's referring to is from the late 1970s into the 1980s, which was definitely a low point for pantomime; it had a distinct whiff of being past its sell-by date. As society was evolving, panto was slow to keep up, and aside from poor production values, there were some pretty offensive stereotypes, whether of gender, race or another kind. With the growing popularity of musicals and the rise of cable TV in the 1980s, pantomime badly needed an overhaul if it was to survive.

## CHANGING TIMES AND WORLD-ALTERING EVENTS

Some changes were less to do with anything problematic and more just certain traditions falling out of common practice. The custom of having women play the Principal Boy, for example, worked in Victorian times when it was still rare to have a woman on stage. But things move on, and the frisson caused by seeing a woman play a male role had pretty much dissolved, despite Cilla Black causing a surge in the genre's popularity following her starring performance in *Aladdin* at the London Palladium in its 1970–1 season. As we moved into the 1990s and early 2000s, there came the rise of soap-star and pop-star boys, whose obsessive fandoms made them sure-fire ticket sellers, so they were natural choices for the Principal Boy roles. Heartthrobs of the time, from *East-Enders*' Paul Nicholls to members of Boyzone and S Club 7, and even ever-popular presenters Ant and Dec, made appearances in pantomimes throughout this period. And it wasn't just the TV and pop-band boys that were showing up on the pantomime stage. Their female counterparts – including Rochelle Humes from The Saturdays and Suzanne Shaw from Hear'Say – also starred, usually as Principal Girls.

By the 2010s, producers were wise to the fact that it paid (literally) to have celebrities who were used to performing on stage, rather than just being a famous face off the TV, and talent shows like *The X Factor*, *Britain's Got Talent* and, yes, *Strictly Come Dancing* proved good places to spot potential panto stars. While becoming more contemporary in its values and representation, pantomime also got back to its *commedia dell'arte* and music hall roots, with proper talented acts who could entertain large live audiences taking on lead roles.

Ultimately, if you don't give the public what they want, if they don't have a great time, they're not going to come back. The need to keep appealing to contemporary audiences has meant pantomime has always had to move with the times, and that's true of casting, the scripts and all aspects of production. Today every single element of pantomimes is given time and close attention so people feel they're getting the quality that they're paying for with their ticket.

If you want to understand how pantomime has become such big business, it makes sense to go to the world's largest pantomime production company: Crossroads. Crossroads, and Qdos before it, were heavily responsible for the professionalisation of pantomime, being strategic in their casting, hiring sharp scriptwriters and insisting on excellent production values. Without throwing out the baby with the bathwater, they managed to shake off the more tired tropes and embarrassingly outdated jokes, and embraced popular culture, skilfully interweaving classic traditions and contemporary trends in a way that made pantomime relevant again.

I've already mentioned Michael Harrison and Jonathan Kiley as being the two people who got me involved in pantomime in the first place, and they are the chief executive and casting director, respectively, of Crossroads. I sat down with both Harrison and Kiley to hear more about the machine that keeps us treading the boards each year, how they got started in panto and how they have seen the world of pantomime change over the years. Harrison first worked in pantomime at the King's Theatre in Glasgow:

*I'd been doing work experience there while I was at university in Edinburgh and I heard that they'd lost their director, so I made an offer of directing the pantomime for £1. I thought it was the only way they'd give me the job as I was only in my twenties. So I said, 'Give me a fee of £1, but if it gets great reviews in both the* Herald *and the* Scotsman, *you can pay me the going rate.' I directed* Sleeping Beauty, *starring the late Gerard Kelly and Elaine C. Smith. Thankfully, it went incredibly well and I was invited back to direct the panto the following year.*

*Nick Thomas, who was running Qdos at the time, came to see the show and offered me a job as executive producer at the company. I started out at a junior level, under people like Paul Elliott, who was the pantomime king. I kind of grew up through the organisation, starting with four shows to run, then the following year I had eight, then Nick offered me the role of managing director and it went on from there. I directed shows in Newcastle, Plymouth, Southampton, then Birmingham – I've directed Brian Conley in pantomime at the Hippodrome there – and various other big productions over the next ten years.*

*Then the Palladium came along and that kind of changed everything. It catapulted me as a pantomime producer and I think its success and the scale of the productions we put on there have helped pantomime in general. And I hope that the work I've done as a producer – both at the Palladium and at other theatres we work with at Crossroads – has raised the standards across the board.*

*Nowadays there are lots of prominent pantomime productions all around the country – Edinburgh, Glasgow, Newcastle, Belfast, Birmingham, and big productions in Southampton, Plymouth and Bristol. The list goes on. And obviously pantomime doesn't need to be bigger to be better: some of the best and most respected shows are in the smaller theatres where the budget might not stretch to much, but if the talent on stage and the material they're working with is strong, then you have a great show.*

Kiley's journey into pantomime, meanwhile, was through the performing side, acting in pantomime for around twenty-five years, before becoming a producer and now a casting director. He has been on both sides of the stage – which undoubtedly is one of the reasons he is such an excellent casting director, as he knows what it takes to win an audience over.

*I loved going to watch panto as a kid: I would sit there for two hours and be taken away into a magical world of make believe. It was such a buzz – I'd go out and buy the sheet music for the pop songs in the pantos I went to see. I've always loved popular entertainment and worked as an actor in musicals and panto for a long time: my first West End show was as Tootles in* Peter Pan *at the London Coliseum, and I performed as Joseph in* Joseph and the Technicolor Dreamcoat *six times. Pantomime was my favourite, though – I used to work my schedule around it and make sure the Christmas season was clear, because it was my obsession.*

*I moved into the production side of pantomime with Paul Elliott at E&B Productions, and then E&B sold to Nick Thomas, becoming Qdos Productions in 1999. Paul left Qdos, as he'd become a producer in his own right, and that was when Michael Harrison came on board. Crossroads at the time was run by David Ian, and he asked Nick if he wanted to sell Qdos to Crossroads as they did musical theatre productions all over the world but didn't have a pantomime arm and were keen to acquire one. He did so, and now Crossroads has been around in its current form for about six to seven years.*

*I'd been producing shows, but when Michael, who adored pantomime as much as I did as a boy, started producing the pantomimes at Qdos, I shifted over to the casting side of things. Because he loves pantomime and all the outrageous, wonderful people who have populated it, like Danny La Rue and Ken Dodd, he just gets it. He really took it to the next level in terms of production values, because that was his big thing. He works on high-profile productions with Cameron Mackintosh and Andrew Lloyd Webber, doing all these mega shows, like* Sunset Boulevard, *etc.*

*We're lucky to have an incredible team, all of us driven by the same obsession with pantomime. It's a joyous cottage industry, really.*

Crossroads has become an unbeatable force. They don't solely produce pantomime, but pantos do make up the vast majority of their UK output, and it is a military operation, with twenty-three to twenty-six shows a year being put on across the UK and Northern Ireland, from Aberdeen to Belfast, Bristol to Newcastle, Bradford to Southend.

Covid was a devastating global pandemic, radically changing the way we all lived and worked, and it's almost unimaginable now to think of the number of lives lost to it. The world as we knew it ground to a halt. And the arena of performing arts was not exempt. Covid did, inevitably, hit theatre, and pantomime within that, badly in the 2019–20 season, with productions either cancelled or postponed to 2021. It was a sad irony that pantomime's greatest strength – its multi-generational audiences – became its Achilles' heel, with the risk to more vulnerable members of the population too great to consider going ahead. The loss of that season's revenue has been estimated at a staggering £90 million,[4] once both ticket sales and secondary sales are factored in. Eden Court in Inverness, the biggest arts venue in the Scottish Highlands, estimated that it alone had lost £350,000 in revenue.[5] The Palladium, initially given the go-ahead for socially distanced performances of *Pantoland*, starring Julian Clary, Elaine Paige, Beverley Knight, Paul Zerdin, Gary Wilmot and Nigel Havers, had to close after six performances when the government moved London into a higher tier of lockdown.

I was meant to be performing as the Wicked Stepmother in *Cinderella* in Southampton at the Mayflower Theatre that season, and then, when that was cancelled, as the Sheriff of Nottingham in a shorter-run performance of *Robin Hood* in Woking, but that too ended up being cancelled as greater restrictions were put in place. Although I've always believed that pantomime can survive even an apocalypse, I can't pretend that I wasn't extremely worried about the impact on the performing arts and the loss of jobs in the industry. Luckily, despite fears that the pandemic would put paid to audiences coming out to see panto, each year since has seen record-breaking attendances, with 2025–6 proving to be yet another unprecedented year for ticket sales. Crossroads' 2025 Palladium pantomime, *Robin Hood*, was the fastest-selling show in its nine-year history. Having faced the potential of a shaky future for the genre only a few years prior, Kiley is delighted to see pantomime continue to thrive:

*It seems to be bucking the trend. Theatre is still struggling, particularly in the provinces since Covid. People were scared to go out and of course we had to remove seats at one point because there had to be social distancing so a very limited number of seats could be used. There was a time when I didn't think we'd ever get back to the numbers we saw pre-pandemic, so to be bringing even larger audiences than before is astonishing.*

The resilience of pantomime in the face of pandemics and economic crises forces those who look down on it as an art form to see its value – even if just in the financial sense. Interestingly, drama schools are clearly savvy to the upside of pantomime economics . . . Principal Girl Elly Jay recalls how in college, she and her fellow students weren't allowed to audition for shows until they'd finished their three years' study. That was, except for pantomimes – as it didn't necessarily matter if they missed the college Christmas Show, which wouldn't affect their curriculum modules. As they were represented by their college agency, the agency would get commission on this. No one's snooty about pantomime when they look at their paycheque, which is handy for casting directors like Jonathan, who go to graduate shows to seek out the very best graduates – the ones they can tell will go on to become big stars.

It's a seemingly unchangeable fact that some people – actors included – are still snobbish about pantomime, despite its undeniable popularity. Or perhaps it's because of that popularity. Daniel Norford, who's appeared in a number of pantomimes now, in roles ranging from Prince Charming in *Cinderella* to the genie in *Aladdin*, compares it to acting in TV soaps:

*I remember being at drama school and we were doing the showcase. Just before the showcase, everyone was going, 'I won't do any soaps.' After the showcase, everyone was saying, 'Just give me any job possible.' And just as soaps are a tough gig, I'd say panto is one of the hardest shows to do and certainly the most underrated.*

Jonathan Kiley believes the success of the Palladium annual pantomime has really opened the genre up to a whole breed of actors who were a bit prissy about it before:

*There are people doing it now just because they went to see a panto at the Palladium and realised it's so much more than they expected, in fact it's the greatest show in London. If you go to see a pantomime, you instantly feel that the rapport between the actors and audience is unique; somehow seeing it on the huge stage at the Palladium makes it even more electric. And it's clear that for the actors to get it right requires such discipline, as much as any play or comedy.*

As I touched on in Chapter 1, the English class system plays a part in the elitist attitude towards both soaps and pantomime. But anyone who has performed in a pantomime knows that it is one of the toughest genres to work in and do well. Stephenson Ardern-Sodje, a newcomer to the form, as I've mentioned, was struck by the rigour of the industry:

*I know musical theatre performers often get referred to as being like athletes and I think panto performers are like the marathon runners of that subset. In musical theatre, you're doing eight shows a week, and you do quite a lot of choreography and singing, but then here we're doing twelve shows a week and the dancers have to be so flexible and strong to sustain that. I did used to say I didn't want to do panto, but then I saw one at the Palladium and was blown away. I suppose it's a bit like back in the day when people would say, 'I'll do film but I won't do TV.' Everything changes. Now, would those same actors do TV? Hell yeah.*

When I ask him why he thinks we're seeing such a surge in love for pantomime, he pauses to reflect:

*It's a safe place where you know that you're going to have a great time. You can see your favourite star in a great show; you know you're going to laugh and have fun. And as producers and directors, we know that simplicity is best: don't have overly long performances – children have the concentration span of half an hour, if you're lucky! – and keep the shows tight and fast. There are no pauses in pantomime; these days, it's about keeping up the energy. Twenty years ago, you'd have a slow ballad thrown in, which was usually when half the audience nipped to the toilet! But now we're competing with all sorts of media, not just streaming TV but the social media apps on people's phones, so we have to keep them focused on what's happening on stage. For example, you need a fantastic number before the interval, maybe with some special effects, like snow coming down on the audience or a carriage being pulled by horses flying over their heads, so that they're excited to come back in and see the rest of the show.*

## A WELL-OILED MACHINE

The shows all feel so effortless and fun that it would be easy to think that they're easy to put on, but these productions are planned to the last detail to ensure that audiences are getting exactly what they came for. Pantomime as a genre has many attributes that keep it eternally popular, but make no mistake, it is not an accident that ticket sales continue to flourish: this is a well-oiled machine whose producers know exactly what panto audiences want to come out and see.

Across their twenty-something pantomime shows each year, Crossroads will have approximately a thousand people working on them, from actors to set and costume designers and lighting managers, assistant stage managers to choreographers . . . Which Kiley notes makes the hotel bill for everyone during panto season huge! And although we all turn out to watch pantomime between November and January, for the people working in the industry it's a year-round job. They release pre-sale tickets for their pantomime shows in March, or even before, which seems extremely early, but even in a cost-of-living crisis, people book for their favourite pantomimes that far in advance. Sometimes that pre-sale moment can shift as much as 60–70 per cent of tickets.

Naturally there are some years where tickets are slower to shift than others, and I know sales are down when I see another celebrity face added to the line-up on the poster of the pantomime I'm in. The marketing team at Crossroads have plans in place to ensure that if, at certain junctures in the year, ticket sales aren't where they need to be, they can release a certain piece of advertising or do a press run and get more seats sold.

Social media is inevitably a big part of marketing the shows these days – collab posts with the celebs starring in each panto get word out to our followers, so it's no longer a case of relying on posters and listings. There will often be behind-the-scenes promotional videos in costume, which introduce the cast to online audiences well before rehearsals actually start, and aim to capture the excitement of the show itself. And of course there's always a press day at the venue. So there are plenty of levers for us to pull to ensure we get the proverbial bums on seats.

While we're on the subject of selling tickets, I was interested to find out how the pricing for these works. It's tricky to establish the average ticket prices for a pantomime show, since there is such a wide range of productions across the country – you might pay a nominal fee for a local village or town production, for example, particularly if it's an amateur show. But you'd expect to pay a lot more for a larger-scale city performance – premium tickets for the London Palladium pantomime can cost north of £250. Who better than Harrison, as CEO of the largest producer of pantomime in the UK, to ask about how the pricing is figured out:

*Well, ticket prices vary from city to city. Of course, there can be very cheap tickets for schools, and higher priced tickets around peak performance times at Christmas. The prices are always set by the producer in conjunction with the theatres. The partnership that we have with the theatres we work with is closer than you might imagine. Other types of shows visit theatres for a week or two weeks a year, but pantomime is the central point of many theatres' programmes, so I work very closely with theatre managers to deliver the kind of show we all want. That can involve anything from casting to setting the price of the ticket. The theatres know their local markets better than anyone, so it makes sense to have such a close partnership.*

Essentially, we work in an ecosystem and factors like the size of the theatre feed into the pricing of the tickets and how many tickets can be sold, which in turn influences the wages of pantomime performers. Broadly speaking, the amount that panto performers get paid has gone up over the last couple of decades, partly due to the Equity minimum wage going up – which impacts all theatre performers – but also thanks to panto's increasing popularity and bankability. Of course, within pantomime there's a whole structure of payment rates, and how much actors are paid depends on other aspects than the size of the theatre. Celebrities do get paid the most, since theatres are relying on them to draw in their fans and ensure tickets sell out. The main or lead characters get paid the most after the celebrity actors, then the chorus actors, playing the more background roles, after that. Those smaller roles are usually played by dancers in their second or third year at college, like Elly Jay was when she first got into pantomime.

Payment is generally a lump sum for the whole pantomime season, which is usually over three or four weeks, depending on the house. If you're at a two-thousand-seater, the run will only have to be three weeks. If you're at an eight-hundred-seater, you have to do four weeks for the same money. I tend to sign a three-year contract to perform in a specific pantomime and play the same part for that stretch, so I don't have to learn something new every October while I'm doing *Strictly Come Dancing*. Thank goodness, or I'd have to lock myself away in the bedroom for four hours each day for it to process and go in.

The intensity of performing so many shows in such a short period of time is a shock to anyone not used to doing it. It's two shows a day, six days a week. Because I record *Strictly* until midnight on a Saturday, that's the company's day off. I remember once finishing work on *Strictly* at 1 a.m., getting straight into a car that drove me to the theatre for 7 a.m., then having my make-up put on at 8 a.m. for a 10 a.m. show, because the theatre did three panto shows on a Sunday. I just couldn't get any sleep with the late finish on *Strictly*, though, so I've had to keep it to two Sunday shows.

In order to put on so many productions, rehearsal times are short and they are extremely efficient – and it's no surprise that you'll see a core of pantomime actors performing each year in Crossroads productions, because they know the drill and can be relied on to jump into action at short notice. There are usually just two weeks of rehearsals for shows: one for dress rehearsals, then another for technical run-throughs for lighting and sound. People freak out because there's so much to learn in so little time.

On Monday afternoon that first week we'll start blocking (i.e. going through our parts in the correct positions on stage); by the end of Tuesday the whole show is roughly blocked; then on Wednesday we go into the detail. If there's a fight scene, we'll have a fight director booked in and we'll often have a separate studio booked for rehearsing dance routines with the dance choreographer, which usually happens on the Thursday. Then, on Friday, it all comes together and by Saturday lunchtime you're ready to go. So it really is all done at lightning pace, which is why it makes sense for panto production companies to work with actors who perform pantomimes year in, year out and are able to get the hang of things quickly.

Although I'm still a celebrity performer in pantomime, I've been doing it so long I now feel like I'm part of the troupe! There's always a great camaraderie and you really can't get away with being difficult, as an actor, when you're working in pantomime – not with the team working on the shows, nor your fellow actors, and especially not with the audience. The people who pay to come and watch shows can sniff out someone who isn't giving it their all and to make it work, you need what Kiley refers to as a 'twinkle with the audience':

*You have to have some sort of generosity of spirit. If you're selfish as an actor, then the audience can tell. Those people don't last long in pantomime. When you've got twenty-three shows together, everyone in the cast has to get on and enjoy each other's company, or the audience will sense that something isn't gelling. If you cast a show correctly, half the job is done. I never do online castings: people send in self-taped auditions all the time these days, but I insist on seeing people face to face; I need to feel what they're like in person and how they're going to interact with other cast members.*

*I worry about the dearth of stars who bring that generosity to the stage. That's why the hunt's always on to find those people who can really captivate an audience. It's not as simple as saying, 'Oh, he's a popular celebrity, let's get him to play in one of our pantomimes this year.' They need to get pantomime as an art form. Will Young did his first panto recently. He completely got it and knew what he had to do; he was just fabulous. No grandness. Panto is such a specialised form and it really requires actors who can be responsive to whatever is happening on the stage as well as in the audience. It's like a tennis match between the actors – they've all got to keep hitting the ball back to each other, keeping a rally going. If someone drops the ball, energy-wise that is, you lose the audience completely and you can't afford that.*

And he notes that it's not just actors that we're in need of for future generations of panto – there are also fewer and fewer directors, he feels, who really understand the sort of energy required by this particular genre. Thankfully, Kiley has an expert eye and manages to spot both the actors and the behind-the-stage talent that will bring in the crowds. If there's a star one year who is new to pantomime, he or another member of the team ensures a very experienced director is on board to get them up to speed quickly. After all, there's no panto school! The only way to learn is on the job. But everyone is made to feel welcome in panto. It's a cliché but it does really feel like a big family.

The actors that the producers use for the main corps of performers have to be really excellent. That's why you'll see a lot of repertory actors or West End leading ladies and leading men in those roles, especially to play the primary parts: high-calibre professionals who can sing, dance and act – and crucially, are likeable. It's not easy to get it right. In fact, it's bloody difficult to get it right, particularly when you've got a thousand people

I've played Captain Hook in *Peter Pan* a few times now, and it's always tremendous fun.

Doing the conga with the lads, as the Wicked Stepmother in *Cinderella*.

WHO did you say was the fairest of all?? Another panto, another wicked stepmother – but this time a queen, in *Snow White*.

Let's be honest, the villains get the best outfits. The Evil Queen in *Snow White* again.

CRAIG REVEL
as The Wicked
NORTH WALES NO.
Media Partner
heart
more music variety

The poster for my very first panto: *Snow White* at Venue Cymru in Llandudno, North Wales, in the 2009–10 season.

It's always a blast doing pantomimes: it seems to attract the loveliest and most fun people – like these guys, Daniel Norford and Solomon Davy, who I performed with in *Cinderella*, Wimbledon, 2023. We're having the best time up on stage, and that's what the audience picks up on. It's infectious!

shouting at you! But like me, a lot of these actors caught the bug and couldn't keep away, as Jonathan Kiley says:

*We've got a lot of regulars who come back every year; they adore it and give it 100 per cent every time. When you find those people it's gold. It's wonderful seeing someone join as the princess or Cinderella and stay for years and years and switch to playing the Fairy Godmother. That's one of the brilliant things about the genre – there are roles to last a lifetime. Lesley Joseph is a prime example of someone who's been in panto for decades – forty-five years, in fact. She's eighty now and is a great exponent of it; she's a proper, serious comedy actress who has a great profile and is always able to bring the audience along with her, whatever role she plays. The thing we're always aiming for is to have a company of actors who gel and have fun together, so that when the audience comes to see them perform, it feels like they're watching the actors have a party that they're joining.*

Just as the stories in pantomime have been updated to reflect the times, so have the types of production that are staged. With a quarter of people in the UK reporting themselves as disabled,[6] it's important that performances are as inclusive and accessible as possible. So today, we put on shows for people with sensory needs, or for younger children who might be scared by the standard productions. These shows are called 'relaxed performances' and they have a very different dynamic to the usual ones – the whole thing is designed to ensure an enjoyable experience for everyone, but without the level of stimulation you normally get at pantomimes.

In relaxed performances, the lights are kept lower, there are no loud noises and the audience is very much free to move around if they need to. There's a reduced seating capacity, usually 50–75 per cent, so it doesn't feel too crowded, break-out rooms are available if anyone needs a breather, and extra staff are on hand to help if required. Although it varies from theatre to theatre, people attending relaxed performances will often get an outline of what will happen during the show the day before, which also details what the venue layout is like, so they know what to expect and can anticipate any issues it might bring up for them.

For these relaxed performances, I edit my script to suit the audience. When you have people watching with different needs, the performance has to be tailored, whether that's because they might be over-stimulated by bright lights or sudden noises, or because they might shout out at what would be seen by some people as 'inappropriate' moments. For those attendees it's wonderful that they get to have a performance where they know no one will be judging them or annoyed, and they can fully relax and enjoy the experience. It's our job up on stage to keep one ear open for the audience and make sure that while we're delivering our performance, we're also not disturbing anyone – we have to be flexible and sometimes cut lines on the fly if we don't think they will work. Some of the comedy might not land as it usually would, so you just have to be really intelligent about your approach to that specific performance or audience.

Signed performances are another example of tailoring to audiences' needs, and these can come in different forms, as Neil Hurst describes:

*I've done pantomimes where there is a signer at the side of the stage – which is probably what most of us are used to seeing at shows or on TV. Then there are also integrated sign performances, where the signer is assigned to you. So you walk around with your signer and you, as the actor, learn little bits of signing as well.*

These signed performances usually use British Sign Language, and captioning is sometimes used too for greater accessibility. The whole point of pantomime is to entertain *everyone*, so these new moves towards inclusivity are a welcome expansion of traditional productions. Where possible, some theatres even look at the timing of shows in order to suit the local demographics – so if they have a predominantly older crowd, for example, they'll aim to have an earlier start time for performances.

The increasing professionalisation of pantomime has led to it being taken more seriously as a credible genre. But while those of us who work in the professional world of pantomime are thankful for its prosperity, I don't think any of us would ever want a world where there isn't also a passionate amateur scene for it. Ultimately, it's the passion of the people involved with pantomime who make it work, whether you're being paid to do it or not. Seeing Jonathan Kiley's face light up the minute he talks about the world he's worked in for decades tells you everything you need to know about what drives him. Yes, the slick outfit that brings exceptionally produced shows to the UK every year is essential to pantomime being such a thriving industry today. But ask Kiley what the key to its success is and his answer has nothing to do with business:

*When it's done properly, pantomime makes an audience experience emotions, and that's why they turn out every year: it's our job to make them laugh and cry, to scare them; to give them a place to shout and boo, but also to make them listen and have those moments of pathos and reflection. And to experience all that together. There's nothing like it.*

GUEST STAR

# BONNIE LANGFORD

Easily one of the most consistently successful people in show business, Bonnie Langford is a classic star in the old-school mould. She can act, sing, dance and do the full range of tragedy and comedy. Famous since her years as a child star – memorably appearing as Violet Elizabeth Bott in *Just William* and Lena Marelli in *Bugsy Malone* – she continues to light up stage and screen, currently starring in *Paddington: The Musical* at the Savoy Theatre in London. A bona-fide pantomime star since the age of fourteen, her most recent role was as the Good Fairy in *Sleeping Beauty* at the Churchill Theatre in Bromley, in 2021.

*You've had such a storied career, both as child star of film and TV and on the stage in West End and Broadway musicals. Do you have a particular love of pantomime that drew you to perform in it?*

When I was a very little girl, up to the age of five or six, my mother used to provide the choreography and dancers for the Richmond Theatre pantomime in West London. I was essentially brought up in that theatre, watching pantomime. I got to see brilliant Dames like Dougie Chapman, Arthur Askey and Stanley Beard, along with many other stars, in old-fashioned, traditional pantomimes. So it's very much part of my DNA.

*Did you get involved yourself at that young age?*

I used to get up on the stage for the song sheet – where they would give the kids presents – all the time. So much so that I had to start giving the presents back. It was part of my introduction to theatre: it made me very comfortable being in a theatre and going up on stage. I'd line up on the steps by the stage in Richmond Theatre as soon as the song sheet was coming up because I knew when it fell in the pantomime. And many years later, that was where I'd film my main scene for *Bugsy Malone*, in that theatre.

*Did you bring any preconceptions about pantomime with you when you started acting in it?*

Not really, having grown up being so immersed in it. I performed in my first pantomime aged fourteen at the Yvonne Arnaud Theatre in Guildford, playing Cinderella with John Noakes and Peter Purves from *Blue Peter*, and it was a very wholesome family pantomime. I was so young they couldn't even have a royal wedding at the end – I had to have an engagement party instead! You can't imagine a fourteen-year-old playing that role today in a show with adults. I'd done a few TV pantomimes too around that time: I was a regular on a series called *Junior Showtime* on which we performed a few, so I fully understood the concept of pantomime and loved it.

*You've played a number of Principal Boy roles over the years – Dick Whittington, Aladdin – but you've also played Cinderella and a number of Fairy roles. Do you have a preference for playing male or female roles, and if so which and why?*

When I started playing male roles, I found them much more fun. The female roles were a bit sappy and drippy. My first venture in playing Principal Boy roles was in *Jack and the Beanstalk* at Plymouth – it was like doing a big musical. It was hard work: I had to do sword fights and flying around – lots of activity, basically – but you can have a lot more fun and be more cheeky in those boy parts.

*In recent years, fewer women have played Principal Boy characters – is that a change you welcome or disagree with?*

I think it's just a natural case of changing with the times. Obviously those gender-role swaps came from a time when women weren't allowed to perform on stage. There isn't the same need for it now and it can cause confusion. I have a funny story from when I was playing Aladdin at Richmond Theatre with Bernard Cribbins, who was playing a particularly masculine-looking Widow Twankey. I was doing a scene where Aladdin decides he wants to see the princess – she's having a parade through the town but no one's allowed to look at her. Aladdin sits in the apple tree and looks at her anyway. Thinking about it now, it's a bit pervy, but there we are. I had to come out of the tree and say hello to the princess and introduce myself. The actress playing her pretends to be shocked and says, 'Oh, you're the boy from the apple tree.' At this point, in the millisecond of silence before my line, a little voice from the audience shouted out, 'No it's not, it's a girl!' The audience laughed hysterically. Bernie Cribbins ran on in full drag as a Dame and said, 'No he's not! I should know, he's my son. I'm his mother.' The place erupted!

*We've both performed in a lot of musicals, and pantomime today does seem to attract a lot of stars from the big West End shows – I didn't expect to find pantomime every bit as exerting as musicals, if not more so. Did you find this too?*

Pantomimes are hard – generally there's a very packed schedule with a lot of extra shows. In a musical you might do eight shows a week; in a pantomime you could do anything up to sixteen, which I have done. When you're doing three shows a day, by the time you get to the second act of the second show, you become mildly delirious. You can't work out if you've already said the lines and start finding the smallest things hilarious. That's my experience of it, anyway! You've also got this extra character who didn't come to rehearsals called the audience. You're breaking the fourth wall a lot, and you have to be in control of that, otherwise it becomes a shouting match and generally the audience will win, even though you have a microphone. Once you've lost control, it's hard to get them back. Pantomime is fabulous training for people – you start to understand how to talk to an audience yet still remain in character and keep the plot on track. There are so many different elements to juggle. You also have a much smaller rehearsal period – it was even shorter in the old days – so it's a very quick learning curve. One of the hardest things to do is to stay well. If you're in charge of the song sheet and getting kids up on stage, it's tricky; they're little germ-breeders. One year the guy playing Buttons in *Cinderella* got chickenpox! But it's fantastic to see a multi-generational audience where grandma, grandad, mum and dad and the children can be out together.

*You've always played the 'good' characters in pantomime – the opposite of me! Have you ever had a hankering to play a villain? And if so, any particular one?*

The villains do have much more fun. I've played the Fairy Godmother a lot and the role can be a bit saccharine, so I always tried to add a bit of cheekiness. I haven't done pantomime for a long time, but I'd love to play a villain. I've played the 'bad' characters in film and TV in recent years, which has been fun to do as I've got older.

*Are there any memories of pantomime that are particularly special for you?*

The things that kids say stay with you, and I experienced one incredible full-circle example of that. When I was playing Peter Pan at Wimbledon Theatre, the theatre manager would bring his son, who was only five at the time, to watch the show. He'd watch it regularly from the back of the circle. One time he came back to see the show with his friend, and when we came to the scene where Peter flies, he turned to his friend and said, 'When they first did this, they used strings, but now they really fly.' Years later, I did a video for *The One Show* about *Bugsy Malone*, explaining that the Richmond Theatre was where we'd filmed my scene. The new theatre manager got in touch and said, 'You probably don't remember me, but . . .' It turned out he was the old theatre manager's son who used to sit and watch *Peter Pan*, and was now a theatre manager himself, at Richmond Theatre! The way pantomime teaches kids the magic of performance and welcomes them to the world of theatre is priceless.

# 5

# A SIGHT FOR SORE EYES (AND EARS)

## HOW THE DAZZLING SIGHTS AND SOUNDS OF PANTO ARE CREATED

Pantomimes today are visual and aural spectaculars, completely on a par with the big West End musicals for their wow factor. If you think of an outing to the panto, as much as anything else, it's the sheer sumptuous look and sound of it all that makes it so special.

I've played in some of the most incredible venues, from Manchester's Opera House to the Bristol Hippodrome, the Theatre Royal Nottingham to the New Wimbledon Theatre. Many of the gorgeous buildings we perform in are either the original specialist music halls built in the late 1800s, or spaces built in the early 1900s to host variety performances, like the London Coliseum – or were very much created in the image of these older buildings.

The stunning original venues were designed with large-scale performance in mind, able to seat hundreds or thousands of people each night. One of the very first of these purpose-built music halls was Lambeth's Canterbury Hall, created by Charles Morton in 1852, which had a capacity of seven hundred. It was such a roaring success that Morton had to make a fifteen-hundred-capacity venue on the same site, which opened in 1856. This hall had more of the features that we are used to seeing in panto venues today – ornate decoration, a balcony, chandeliers, and food and drink on sale. And the stage sets became increasingly bold and beautiful to match. The more luxurious the feel of the experience, the more audiences could be charged for tickets. This model inspired many imitations, and in time Morton became known as the 'Father of the Halls'.

While it's not so surprising that we still frequently use the buildings from this era, given they were built for this purpose, what may be more surprising is that the visual look of pantomime on stage hasn't really changed that much either. The 'transformation scene' – a change of scenery and/or costume used to dramatic effect – has been part of pantomimes since the eighteenth century, but it's the Victorians we have to thank for really turbocharging this aspect of the production. The innovations of one man in particular, William Roxby Beverly, are largely responsible for the impressive displays we see today. Beverly was an artist and theatrical scene painter who worked as scenic director in a number of iconic London venues, including the Lyceum from 1847, the Covent Garden Opera House – then known as the Royal Italian Opera House – from 1853 and Drury Lane from 1854 (with some overlap in these roles) and developed incredible techniques, pioneering transformation scenes. His real breakthrough moment came during his time at the Lyceum, where he used exciting new techniques, including pivoting stages, to make his shows a visual extravaganza. It was these innovations that really led to pantomimes being regarded as spectacles, so when you see a coach and horses flying above your head in the theatre, he's partly to thank.

The staging of a pantomime is mapped out well in advance of the Christmas run – and for Crossroads, it's usually modelled on their big Palladium show, which becomes a template for the other productions across the country. Of course, there have to be tweaks depending on the venue each show is being performed in, and the particular actors performing. Different comics, for example, will have their own routine, so might need a specific space to operate in; I always have a dance routine as part of my role as the villain, so that's accounted for in the planning. When Pamela Anderson appeared in *Aladdin* at the New Wimbledon Theatre in 2009, she was lowered onto the stage on a swing made from a surfboard. You can't base that on any other show; it's solely about what's right to showcase her and ensuring the audience who have come to see her get to be in on the joke, so there has to be a specific set created to accommodate that moment.

Among my favourite moments in any show is the use of a crane to depict something flying through the air. In *Cinderella* that might be a coach and horses that soars over the audience's heads. Yes, it's actually carried on a giant metal arm, but to the audience, the effect is magical. A little less magical for Gavin Whitworth, however, who, as musical director, is usually in the pit when this special effect is operated: 'Some years they turn it upside down and I hope they're strapped in, otherwise I'm going to be in trouble.'

Crossroads' CEO Michael Harrison feels the most significant changes in the time he's worked in pantomime have really been those in the standards of special effects:

*Of course, special effects are not new to pantomime. In the Victorian days, effects using the machinery of the time were paramount to the success of the productions, but then it all faded away and pantomime did get a bit cheap and – dare I say – a bit tired. But working with companies like The Twins FX has meant we have been able to raise the standards and give spectacular endings to first acts, which hadn't been seen prior to my arrival in pantomime.*

Based in Wareham and run by professional magicians and – surprise, surprise – identical twins, Gary and Paul Hardy-Brown, The Twins FX is the very best when it comes to special effects, animatronics and illusions in theatre. They've also worked with Disney on films, including *Beauty and the Beast* and *The Lion King*. You want a terrifying, giant crocodile able to swallow Captain Hook whole for *Peter Pan*, a breathtakingly stunning carriage and horses that can fly for *Cinderella*, or a floating magic carpet for *Aladdin*? They're the ones to go to. For the 2023–4 London Palladium production of *Jack and the Beanstalk*, The Twins FX created the world's largest pantomime giant: called Nipper Norm, he stands just under ten feet high. That giant crocodile? There are two of them ready for panto season: Bill and Pete.

Another crucial aspect that determines the impact of a pantomime is one that sometimes can be forgotten, ironically *because* it's such an integral part of every show: the lighting. To learn more about it, I spoke to Richard G. Jones, who has been lighting pantos for forty years – twenty-two of those at York's Theatre Royal. He lights between two and four pantomimes a year, depending on what is practical with the shows' locations and their production periods and opening-night timings. I was keen to know what he thought was most important for anyone who does pantomime lighting to keep in mind. It was the magic of the genre that he instantly flagged:

*Panto is a very important part of most theatres' year, and it is often a child's first experience of theatre, so it should be magical. Obviously, most importantly, I look at lighting the actors' faces, so there can be clear dynamic interaction with the audience. We often light the audience during a direct address to them, so they, too, feel part of the action.*

*I treat it like a musical – I really think that the lighting for panto brings in a mix of all genres of theatre, but with a very musical theatre feel. If you think about it, they contain scenes, dance, music and song. So the lighting rig needs to contain a dance side-light, which provides interesting texture, and a back light, to give shape to each scene and also, when needed, to highlight the different pieces of scenery. Use of bold colours in panto is exciting, so it's important to choose colours that work with each number and make each scene and song thrilling for the audience.*

Like everyone involved in professional pantomime, Richard doesn't get much time to pull everything together for a show – he'll often just have three days to light the stage before the show opens, so prep work is vital:

*I have to do a lot of music and script preparation to achieve all the work in a short timeframe. If it's a new panto, I like to be involved at an early stage, i.e. from the point the sets are designed. Many pantos now have a lot of set lighting incorporated, so being there early to talk through ideas and products with the design team is crucial. That being said, for some pantos with a pre-built set, I will only get the photos, ground plans, script and music and so on maybe six weeks in advance. Then it is a fast turnaround to draw a rig plan and get it costed, so decisions are made based on the photos and the script. We have one production meeting with all the creatives and go through everything then.*

Being flexible in the face of changing circumstances is vital for anyone who wants to do Richard's job. Although most of the pantos he's worked on don't tour, that doesn't mean that the lighting doesn't have to be adaptable.

*Once I worked on a York Theatre Royal panto in traverse [where the audience sits facing each other on opposite sides of the stage], but inside a purpose-built tent, as the theatre renovation project had overrun. That one certainly made all the creatives think outside the box! Budget is also a big consideration as you look at lighting the show, so while you're looking to bring added eye candy and special effects, you need to work within the financial remit you've been set.*

Special effects and lighting are a huge part of the visual wow factor of pantomime. The magic factor, however, is often injected by the beauty of the sets.

## TAKING THE SCENIC ROUTE

I'm always amazed by how pantomime sets instantly manage to conjure a fairy-tale-like atmosphere, before any action takes place on the stage. That effect isn't an accident. It comes from the skill and experience of incredible craftspeople: set designers.

I've been lucky to work with some of the best in the business, including the brilliant Mark Walters. Mark was the first set designer to be nominated for an Olivier Award for a pantomime set design, for his work for *Jack and the Beanstalk* at the Palladium (2022–3). He designs sets for theatre of all kinds, including opera, musicals and plays as well as pantomime, and runs the company Glitter Pantomimes, which he founded with Martin Holland in 2010. In some ways it's not surprising, but I was nevertheless quite startled to learn that even set designers face snobbery over working in pantomime. Mark himself has experienced condescension from producers and directors, and recalls a director who told him 'there's one too many pantomimes on here for my liking' after seeing his CV. So that snooty attitude to panto is not just something we performers have to deal with.

Thankfully, Mark ignored the naysayers and his company is hugely successful. He owns a football-sized warehouse full of his sets, costumes and props. Like any kind of artist, a large part of his success and his credibility lies in his distinctive style. 'There are a number of us set designers out there,' he says, 'and every designer has their own style and look. I've got to the point now where I can take one look at a set and know who designed it.' When it comes to his own aesthetic, he says it is 'traditional in many ways':

*I keep it flat but use lots of layers that go deep on the stage, and I use cut-cloths [large cloths with scenes painted on them, which feature cut-outs], which is very much in the panto tradition. I never want to go so modern with it that the traditional aspect is lost. There are some designers who do a contemporary look, some cartoon-style, some painterly. Some do it entirely digitally. Each has its place in the market. I just like to keep it traditional because those sets are why I fell in love with pantomime as a child. I either build fresh designs or buy sets back from the venues I've made them for and put them into storage, revamp them and hire them out later on. That business has snowballed over the last sixteen years. I have twenty-six Christmas shows that go out each year and I do the big Palladium one, which is the largest in pretty much every way – budget, cast size, the stage . . .*

Those stunning sets need a place to be stored for the rest of the year when they're not in use. Crossroads also has a massive set warehouse – theirs is in Beverley in Yorkshire – where scenery, props and lighting and sound equipment are kept, as well as being mended and sometimes even made from scratch. And every year, come panto season, they're loaded up into lorries and sent to whichever theatre they're needed at.

It's easy to see why the London Palladium uses Mark to design sets for its big panto shows – audiences respond to the classic look, which harks back to that fairy-tale atmosphere. As I mentioned, the Palladium show often acts as a template for productions across the country, and it's Mark's job to ensure the set for that big London show can be recreated to work in theatres of different shapes and sizes around the country: 'The Palladium stage is really wide, so I have to design sets that fit but can also be scaled down, because they get dismantled and used across Britain for other shows. For example, the portals [a sort of scenic frame] are designed so that they can be stretched to fit all sizes of stage and lowered, for the same reason, so the scenic elements can work in each venue.'

Michael Harrison notes that the fact the physical production of the Palladium pantomime outlives its season in London and can be packed up to transfer to Birmingham, Southampton, Plymouth and other major cities is a huge boon: 'The capacity for the Palladium to deliver incredible sets and great production values in a scalable way means the regional theatres get to benefit immensely: it is one of the great assets of having the Palladium pantomime.'

That ability to adapt Mark's sets means that as well as creating the sets for the largest show in the UK, he also does so for some of the smallest ones. At Christmas, his name is all over the place. Pantomimes do have some scenes where the set designs are interchangeable – maybe it's a woods scene that works for *Sleeping Beauty*, *Snow White* and *Babes in the Wood* – but each also has its specific requirements – *Cinderella*, for instance, has a kitchen scene and the grand ball – so it's a hell of a lot of work. Understandably therefore, producers like to work with designers they know and trust, because it helps to have a shorthand, as Mark knows:

*On some pantomimes, the set design is very script-oriented and you have to stick closely to what's written, but on others, especially where I have a long-standing relationship with the production companies, they tell me what title they're doing and let me come to the table with my own ideas. And sometimes those ideas can influence the script in turn. I try not to repeat anything, design-wise. Every time there's a new script it will be slightly different because everyone wants to put their spin on it. That said, there are only so many versions of a kitchen you can do! I've done hundreds of pantomime set designs over the years, so it does get harder and harder to come up with something completely fresh.*

Mark starts with loose sketches and then pulls together drawings to show what he's thinking. Once the director and creative team are on board, he turns those into white card models of the kind that architects use. The director and choreographer might tweak them, before Mark takes them away and creates a finished model with coloured-up artwork, which he then presents to the whole team. Once that's signed off, it goes to the builder along with Mark's technical drawings. For a show as big as the Palladium, he says, that process takes over a year from start to finish, with him working on it most days. A panto isn't just for Christmas.

The casting does influence the sets, but obviously that kicks in a bit later, as the starring roles often aren't confirmed at the stage the scripts are signed off and sets have to be planned. So the scenery will be drawn up, and adaptations will then be made to reflect the personalities of the star actors once they're cast. You clearly have to be flexible and patient to do Mark's job: 'In some cases, we'll have got all the way down the line and built the sets, and they'll cast a star last minute and the director or producers suddenly don't want certain sets any more.'

As well as personalising the sets, there's also the wear and tear that happens during the run of productions. We actors can't always gracefully flit around the sets without touching them or messing them up, so they take a battering over the years – sorry about that, Mark! Those sets might be used for up to three shows a day, and as well as actors, there are dancers moving around a lot, and people rushing on and off stage, moving props around from the wings. Given all this, the sets need a fair amount of maintenance.

While set designers do get involved in the special effects, there are also companies who have expertise in that particular area. At the Palladium, for example, Mark will say how he wants the special effects to look – the aesthetics and style of them – and then a special effects company is hired to produce them. But for smaller venues, he'll do them himself. In fact, he often designs the costumes and props as well as the sets. That way, he explains, there is a consistent look, creating what he calls 'a coherent world', rather than something that risks appearing more like patchwork.

While Mark works alone for much of the process, he has a close team of assistants to help him produce the model and drawings. When it comes to the building of his sets, he prefers to collaborate with workshops that produce everything, and who know his style and his favoured scenic artists. 'I'm only as good as the people who produce my designs,' he says. 'They take my little models and reproduce them twenty-five sizes larger. Sometimes you give that artwork to two different workshops and they create two very different versions. So you have to make sure you work with the one you know can realise your vision.'

But he notes there are fewer workshops than there used to be. Covid not only kept a lot of theatres closed over repeated lockdowns, it also damaged a lot of businesses involved in the production side of theatre, some of which didn't recover, even as the pandemic was brought under control. And with those that did continue, many had to cut back on staff, so can no longer take on as many build jobs as they used to. Mark also says the talent exodus to TV and film is an issue, particularly with scenic artists, because there's simply more money in those industries.

Thankfully for directors, producers, actors and audiences alike, though, Mark himself has continued to work in pantomime. While he creates sets for all the shows, he does admit to having a favourite, *Aladdin*, due to its sheer variety of locations. It makes a change, he says, from the village–woods–castle sets of *Cinderella*, *Mother Goose* or *Sleeping Beauty*. And, he adds, in recent years, there has been more cultural sensitivity around the staging of *Aladdin*, to ensure the locations aren't generic and aren't offensive to any culture.

For Mark, the hardest pantomime story to design sets for is *Dick Whittington*, where there are scenes on board a ship, some below deck and some on deck, and a shipwreck scene. There's also a London scene featuring a large shop. The problem with these set-heavy scenes is that the wings are always cluttered: when the ship isn't needed, that set has to be kept just offstage for when it is. This might be one of the reasons *Dick Whittington* isn't put on so much these days.

Like Mark's reference to the cultural sensitivity around *Aladdin*, there have been other necessary changes to keep up with the times – one of these being health and safety regulations, which are *a lot* tighter than when either Mark or I started out. Today, everything has to be risk assessed and signed off before a production can go ahead. In the Palladium shows, Mark says, the council has to be involved and they can say no to any elements of the staging they don't deem safe.

## FACING THE MUSIC

Thankfully there's less risk assessment required on the music side of things . . . There is more original music in pantomime today than there used to be in the past – specially written, West End musical-style tracks – despite it still being heavily reliant on pop songs. In the productions that Crossroads puts on, the musical pieces apart from the pop tracks are usually written by musical supervisor Gary Hinds. The opening number of the show is always an original, and he also composes short pieces that accompany dramatic moments of plot. When rehearsals are running, there will always be a moment or two where the actors are moving across the stage or there's a pause in dialogue and we need some filler music so it's not silent. That's when musical director Gavin Whitworth will contact Gary and see if he or another musical supervisor has anything that might fit, and if not, if they can whip something up that will work.

The lyrics to the original songs that Gary writes for pantos are generally penned by Alan McHugh. He writes a lot of the scripts for the Crossroads pantomimes, too, so he instinctively knows what's needed, dramatically speaking, from the songs.

I've already mentioned how modern productions use pop songs as the main musical element of the show, to keep them feeling current and so the audience can sing along. Meetings are held throughout the year to select the songs that will work best, and these are far from flippant decisions. Ideally, you want a mix of classic tracks that everyone knows – for example, Jonathan Kiley says Steps songs are perfect for panto, because everyone knows the tunes, they're the right length, and they're easy to sing and dance to – and so well known to the audience. In 2025 we had 'APT' by Rosé and Bruno Mars, which the kids went wild for, and we altered the lyrics to say 'Our Party', instead of 'APT'. Actress Alicia Belgarde told BBC Newsbeat that there was one song with a very high-pitched solo that she and her friends were anxious would crop up in the pantomimes they were in in the 2025–6 season: 'I've got so many friends that are in different pantos across the UK and we're all going, "What songs have you got? Have you got 'Golden' from *K-Pop Demon Hunters*?"'[1]

Back in the early days of pantomime, the music was performed completely live, whether just by a pianist, or a small band, or more of a chamber group. Today, it's usually a mixture of recorded music and a handful of live musicians: a bass guitar player, drummer, trumpeter and reed/wind player, who tends to play saxophone and either oboe/clarinet or flute and swaps between that and the sax. To supplement the recorded music that's played over the speakers, we use what are called 'click tracks'. Over to musical director Gavin Whitworth to explain how these work:

*The recorded music plays on a track, and the musicians have earphones through which we can hear a click to help us stay in time with the music. It's literally a click, like a metronome making sure we keep time. It gets quite annoying sometimes! The Palladium has a much larger band than the other shows. They still use some click tracks, but they do have a good number of musicians playing live throughout the show, so are less reliant on them for bulking out the sound.*

Pantomime scriptwriter Vikki Stone, who has a classical music background and training, feels strongly that the musical aspect of pantomime is vital to the overall experience:

*One of my favourite parts of writing panto is choosing the songs. I always look for a good palette of tunes that serve the whole audience (not necessarily all at the same time). I also try to ensure that most of the songs move the story forward, and that some carry real emotional weight. I treat the inclusion of songs in the same way I would when writing a musical; I give it the same level of thought and craft.*

It's this sort of joined-up thinking that ensures the pantomimes you go to see today are such incredibly slick productions, with no aspect of the stagecraft left to chance and every part of the whole working just as hard as the others. As a consequence, the shows are unbeatable pieces of entertainment.

## ALL DRESSED UP

One of the most fun aspects of performing in panto – and simultaneously one of the most frustrating, at times – is the costumes. My outfits as the Evil Stepmother in *Snow White* are stunning but take ages to get in and out of! These incredible clothes, however, can really help us get into character. Elly Jay remembers some advice she was given on that score:

*My singing teacher told me that I should always wear the shoes I'm performing in when I'm practising. If I was rehearsing songs for a show, he would say, 'Do you have the same footwear on right now that you will in performances?' Inevitably I'd be wearing my trainers. And he'd say, 'Well put a pair of stilettos on. If you're performing in stilettos, put them on while rehearsing, because it changes your whole frame and how you stand.' And it's true: once I put those heels on, I'm in Cinderella mode.*

Crossroads has a wardrobe department of eight or so women working throughout the year to repair and furbish costumes. Thanks to their budgets, the Palladium shows can afford new costumes for their shows, but for most venues, they're kept and worn for as many years as they last. Some of the costumes are worn across a number of different pantomimes: for example, the prince in one panto looks exactly the same as the prince in another – there isn't the specificity that's needed to portray Snow White or Cinderella. Princes are ten a penny, let's be honest.

Lesley Brown has worked as a Wardrobe Supervisor and costume maker for over thirty years. When most plays come to the theatre she works at, the Theatre Royal Nottingham, costumes arrive ready-made, but with pantomimes, she and her team have more of an opportunity to get stuck in. Some of the costumes, like the Cinderella dress she shows to me as we're talking, have been worn in numerous productions – sometimes for over a decade. Recycling like this makes complete sense, given the productions feature the same characters every year, but it can throw up some . . . well, *sensory* issues, as Lesley says:

*Because the costumes have been used year in, year out, the actor is inevitably stepping into clothes that have been sweated in by someone else, night after night . . . Due to the textiles stage costumes are made of – very few are non-polyester – there are a lot I won't be able to wash. Whatever I can wash, I do, every day of a show's run. And then I insist that the dressers spray everything else after every evening show. We do steam sometimes, but the steam tends to bring out the smell. Once they step out on the stage it's fine: they're in make-believe land there, and can imagine they're smelling of roses!*

Occasionally, a new costume is needed, which is a fun moment for the wardrobe team – they have to follow the vision of the producer or director, of course, but it's a moment for their creative juices to get flowing.

As with most of the other elements of pantomime, the wardrobe side of things is very much a case of long-term planning, followed by a breakneck leap into action just ahead of the panto season. This last year, Lesley and her assistant, Helen Guy-Clark, attended rehearsals on Monday and Tuesday two weeks before the show to do fittings and alterations, then on Wednesday hit the shops for any additional bits and pieces, and went back to the theatre to get the dressing rooms ready for when the director, producers and actors (myself included) returned at the weekend. Then it was run-throughs during the following week, dress rehearsal on the Friday and lights up on the Saturday.

If two weeks seems like a short time, that's not the half of it, Lesley says, noting how actors have a tendency to throw a spanner in the works . . .

*I can guarantee that half of the costumes will still need tweaking in those last few days, or the actors will go out on stage and dance and tread on their clothes and tear them. So they're back in the dressing room with me having to stitch them back up.*

*One year, one of the male dancers kept coming back to us in wardrobe, because his trousers kept falling down. We just could not get them to fit. As a dancer, you need them to stretch, but obviously they need to stay up, too. We worked it out in the end, thankfully, or the audience would have got more than they'd bargained for.*

Asked what the essentials are in wardrobe, she'll tell you it's a sewing machine and a glue gun. That and, in a newer twist, the Kimble gun – a device used in shops to add tags to clothes. If something needs a quick repair during a performance, Lesley grabs the Kimble gun to hold the item together and the actor can go back on stage until there's time to take it away and do a proper repair. It's their secret weapon.

Christina Bianco knows the importance of getting used to your costume so you can avoid any on-stage disasters – with those short rehearsal times, it's essential we quickly get to know the stage and how we're going to navigate it. Doing rehearsals in jeans and trainers would have meant that Christina, who had to wear heels and a dress for her role as the Fairy Godmother in *Cinderella*, knew her blocking, but not, for example, that the corner of her dress would catch on a particular piece of set if she didn't hitch it at a certain moment. 'Everything is heightened in a panto,' she observes, 'and the wardrobe and the props are more extreme than in most theatre productions.'

*There are a lot of things you really will not understand how to fully implement and integrate into your show until you start running the show in full costume. All the little things you can do in the rehearsal room to take one bit of uncertainty off the list and to make you feel confident can make a big difference. So yes, I'll hold the wand and yes, I'll wear the heels and dress, even if everyone else is in sweatpants and trainers! I'm a four-foot-eleven woman, so I'm not a stranger to high heels, but if you're wearing heels in the show, you need to know how the stage boards will feel underneath you. I ask wardrobe to borrow my gown underskirt for as long as I can, because it's the lowest-hanging part of my costume and if I'm stepping on and off benches, the last thing I need is to trip up on the night. It's best to find out ahead of time that you need to pick it up.*

As for me, I'm spoiled: I'm lucky in that, like other celebrity performers in panto, my costumes are custom-made. They're not always new for each run – I might have worn them a previous year – but they have been tailored to fit me. Having our own costumes doesn't mean we celebs are immune to wardrobe malfunctions, though . . . At the Bristol Hippodrome in 2022, when I was playing the Evil Stepmother in *Cinderella*, my wig fell off. I had a second of going, 'Oh my God!' in my head, and saw everyone on stage had burst out laughing – Cinderella, the prince, Dandini . . . It went down so well with the audience that we worked it in as part of the show.

At the very end of a pantomime, after the song sheet, there's always something called a 'walkdown'. This is where the whole cast comes out to take a bow, with the Principal Boy and Girl being the last to return to the stage. Everyone wears a fresh change of clothes for this final appearance. One year we all came out wearing pink – having us all wear clothes in the same colour, or with a similar look, really makes it a wonderfully democratic moment as we greet the audience's applause together.

Another respect in which everyone is equal in panto is that we all do our own make-up, me included! There's no sitting in make-up – we have to get out our own kits and create the faces you see up on stage. You only get your make-up done if you have a specialised prosthetic, and even then only if there's a budget for it.

I tour with my own make-up kit, and the look changes from character to character. The last character I played, the Wicked Stepmother in *Cinderella*, has a costume that's all purples and greens, so the make-up needs to complement that. For the more dramatic characters like the Wicked Queen in *Snow White*, meanwhile, you want to look more Disney-esque and evil, with a very dark, sinister brow and very manicured cheekbones. I was taught drag make-up when I did *La Cage aux Folles* in 1985 – drag is one of the few forms of performance that have make-up as outrageously loud as in pantomime – and learned how to wax out my eyebrows and things like that. Nowadays there are YouTube demonstrations that teach you how to do it all. You can literally go online and find a tutorial for 'How to do the Wicked Stepmother's make-up from *Cinderella*', it's that specific.

Personally, I prefer to work it out myself. It's trial and error, knowing what suits your face and what will read over the footlights. The hardest thing for newer performers in panto to get used to is how over the top the make-up has to be. I remember Jonathan Kiley saying one time, 'Everyone needs to do their make-up as dramatically as Craig is doing his: the Ugly Sisters look too pretty!' They have to have grotesque eyebrows and put on ridiculous amounts of rouge, so when they say, 'Aren't we gorgeous?', everyone in the audience shouts, 'No!' If the actors playing those roles do look gorgeous, the comedy falls flat. The bigger and bolder and more expressive the better. Unless you're the Principal Girl, of course. And what's fun about doing the make-up is that you can change it up. You know, on a daily basis, if I get bored, darling, I might do a brown lip line and a pink lip.

## DANCING THE NIGHT AWAY

While I'm always happy to handle my own make-up for panto, one thing I don't normally get involved in is the choreography, even though I've choreographed a lot of other shows in my career. In fact I've only ever choreographed one pantomime, and it was one I was starring in, *Snow White and the Seven Dwarfs*.

The choreography for pantomimes is often determined by the dance skills of the actors. If your leads are better actors and singers than dancers, then the main numbers will be simplified, but if they've come from musical theatre – like myself! – and have more ability in that area, the choreographers have a lot of space to come up with entertaining and impressive pieces. It's not quite like a musical, where there is almost constant dancing, but what elements of dance there are within a panto production are always woven neatly into the storyline. There is definitely a lot of cross-pollination between pantomimes and musicals these days, which Michael Harrison believes is a positive for both genres: 'It's great when people from the West End want to work in pantomime and vice versa. They're both big productions which require a lot of time and effort and particular skill to get right. I feel musicals and pantomimes can learn from each other.' So it's no surprise that he has had Karen Bruce, who has considerable experience of West End musicals, choreographing the London Palladium shows in recent years. Because it's the biggest pantomime of the year, the Palladium show's choreography – like all aspects of its productions – has to be world-class. Bruce is an Olivier Award-winning choreographer who has worked extensively in TV and film, and across a broad range of incredible stage shows, from *The Bodyguard* musical to *Brighton Rock* at the Almeida, and from *Pacific Overtures* at the Donmar Warehouse to choreographing *Strictly Come Dancing* for five seasons from 2011. Her experience in those big musicals makes her the perfect person to produce suitably ambitious dance sequences for the Palladium's large stage – especially for the song sheet.

The song sheet is really the main dance piece of the whole show in pantomime, so choreographers have more to play with there, and they will also usually choreograph the walkdown – although it isn't necessarily an all-out dance number; it is more a coordinated and elegant piece of movement. The actors all need to know when to run up to take their bow, and when to return to join the rest of the company. It all looks very natural, but is actually timed immaculately so no one gets in the way of anyone else.

The reason I don't tend to do panto choreography myself is because these days it's heavily reliant on street style, which isn't really my area of dance. And more than ever now, it's about keeping up with the latest dance trends when it comes to what numbers are put into the shows. Throughout the year it's down to the producers, directors and choreographers to be up to date on what's trending in pop culture and on social media. TikTok dance trends are increasingly finding their way into panto performances because the children love seeing things they recognise, and they're more likely to enjoy the show.

It's part of the challenge for everyone involved in the business side of pantomime to ensure that it continues to reflect society. The dancers help with that a lot, as they're usually in their late teens or early twenties, so are very much aware of what younger people are into. They come to work bringing a wealth of material that they've seen on TikTok or Instagram or wherever, and the producers and choreographers then draw on that for the shows. One year flossing was all over TikTok, so suddenly the choreography for that year's pantomime had to include flossing. And kids get bored pretty quickly, so every year it's something different. You can't give them old-fashioned choreography.

I suppose, in many ways, social media just picked up where MTV left off – and we're still doing the same thing, taking what is trending in youth culture and weaving it into our shows. Social media is even more relentlessly fast-paced than MTV, though, and trends come and go in the blink of an eye. Sometimes it's only when the parents and grandparents see these dances in pantomimes that they understand what it is their kids have been talking about all year. 'Why are all the kids saying six, seven?' Well, come to panto and it'll be in there somewhere, so you can understand what they're on about!

GUEST STAR

# PETE FIRMAN

One of the best-loved comics and magicians in the country – appearing on numerous TV shows, including BBC1's *The Magicians*, ITV's *Don't Unleash the Beast* and Amazon's *Good Omens* – Pete Firman has also become a firm favourite treading the pantomime boards.

He made his professional pantomime debut in *Snow White and the Seven Dwarfs* at the Churchill Theatre in Bromley in 2017. Thankfully for us, he hasn't looked back, but weaves his mind-boggling sleight of hand tricks into the roles he plays, and always manages to bring belly laughs to every production. I caught up with him to find out more about his path into the genre.

*How did you get into pantomime and did you come to it with any preconceptions?*

I was approached by a pantomime producer to do my first one. It wasn't something I'd really thought about getting into, to be honest, but magic and comedy really is a perfect fit for it. I'd always been a fan of it: I've got very fond memories of family trips to our local pantomimes when I was a kid, so the idea of appearing in one appealed and I jumped at the chance.

*Did you find it useful to draw on your experience as a comedian and magician when doing pantomime? I came to it through musicals and was amazed that pantomime is every bit as physically taxing, if not more so.*

Absolutely. All of the elements I employ in my usual work are invaluable in pantomime. Comedy of course, both verbal and physical. But also audience participation, which is such a huge part of pantomime, is something I do all the time. Magic, too, can drop seamlessly into a pantomime as the whole thing is make-believe.

*As a comic and magician it makes sense that you've played the Silly Billy, Buttons and Muddles roles, which involve the most interaction with the audience of any part. Are you ever nervous about how the audience will react?*

I'm never really nervous about interacting with an audience. There's always such fun in the air at a pantomime and I think everyone arrives knowing the rules. They cheer for the goodies and boo for the baddies and they realise that they are going to be involved and interacted with. They're ready to experience that and even if unexpected things occur, they enjoy seeing me deal with those moments and recognise that this thing has never happened before; it's a funny improvisation just for them.

*You're resident comic at New Wimbledon Theatre – do you find that gives you a special dynamic with the pantomime audience when the season comes around, which someone coming from out of the area might not have?*

It's a very special thing. In a funny sort of way, I feel like that theatre is my front room, I'm totally at home there. I look forward to seeing the audiences come back each year and I like to think at least some of them look forward to seeing me!

*So far you've always played the good guys – do you have a hankering to play a panto villain? And if so, which one would you choose?*

I'm afraid I have no hankering! I love playing the comic roles. I love the relationship with the audience and I like getting laughs too much – the boos just don't do it for me!

*How do relaxed performances differ for you as a performer who would usually be very involved with the audience? Do you have certain things you do differently?*

I always cut out any individual interaction. I feel like talking to the audience as a whole is fine, but as I don't know anybody's circumstances, I think it's best not to pick on anyone or interact directly. I also ignore any noise from the audience, which ordinarily I'd respond to and try to find a funny moment in. The relaxed performance is often a very different show to the rest of the run, but for me it's no less enjoyable.

*If you had one piece of advice for someone appearing in pantomime for the first time, what would it be?*

Keep your eyes and ears open. You'll be surrounded by people with many years' experience at doing it. Just listen, learn and take it all in.

*And last but not least, do you have a favourite pantomime, and does it differ depending on whether it's your favourite to star in vs your favourite to watch?*

I think *Cinderella* is my favourite. Buttons is, in my opinion, the best role for a comic. He's got a real story arc and there's pathos as well as the laughs. I always enjoy playing him. I think it's my favourite to watch as well – it's got it all. I suppose that's why it's a classic.

# 6

# THE PLAY'S THE THING!

## FROM IMPROV TO SCRIPTED STAGE SHOWS

The scriptwriting of pantomime is perhaps where I should have started this book. After all, without it, there isn't really panto in the form we know it today. And yet it was a part of the genre that came as a relatively late piece of the puzzle. As I touched on earlier, because pantomime was derived from improvisational forms, the art of panto scriptwriting wasn't properly developed until the Victorian era – again, as a result of the 1843 Theatres Act permitting spoken drama outside venues with a royal patent.

It was during this period that the contributions of J. R. Planché and Edward Litt Laman Blanchard, who we met in Chapter 1, came to the fore, along with the work of other writers, such as Mancunians Henry Byron – magazine editor, playwright and second cousin to *that* Byron (poet and lord) – and William Wade, who alongside writing pantomimes was deputy editor for the *Manchester Times*. Like Planché and Blanchard, Byron and Wade were among the scriptwriters who based their pantomimes on fairy tales.

But what other aspects, beyond this focus on fairy stories, are found in the genre's scripts and make up the bedrock of panto as we know it today?

## THE KEY ELEMENTS

With today's scriptwriters having to draw together classic fairy-tale plotlines, panto catchphrases, multi-level gags, pop-culture references, local in-jokes and audience-interactive dialogue, it's no wonder the role is often split up among a team. But while the scripts have become increasingly complex over the years, they have thankfully retained some music hall raucousness too. Today we tend to think of the Victorians as being uptight prudes, but as in any age with a lot of censorship and moral puritanism, there was pushback, and there was plenty of rude and ribald entertainment if you were looking for it. It's the Victorians and their music hall performers to whom we owe the classic panto catchphrases, like 'He's behind you' and 'Oh no, he isn't/Oh yes, he is'.

The structures of pantomime scripts don't tend to apply any hard-and-fast rules, other than the fact they're in two acts, each usually with an intro scene (or a 'Prologue' to Act 1), and split by an interval so everyone can nip to the loos and top up their refreshments. And of course there is always the 'song sheet', which I mentioned earlier – the part of the show where everyone sings along and, in the past, a lot of children from the audience were invited up on stage.

Beyond that, the scenes follow a pattern that is dictated by staging, alternating between full-stage scenes and scenes that are performed at what is called the 'front cloth'. Front cloth scenes, unsurprisingly, take place in front of a painted curtain (the cloth) while the sets are changed behind it. It's usually a comedic or audience participation scene that happens 'front cloth', or one where a character is on the road – when the prince is travelling to the overgrown palace in *Sleeping Beauty*, for example – maintaining the momentum while the necessary stage adjustments are made. The full-stage scenes, meanwhile, are where the big set pieces and main action in the script occur.

More than structure, however, the key factor in a good pantomime script is sharp and thoughtful storytelling and knowing what will connect with audiences. At the heart of this is something we've already alluded to: the tailoring of jokes to wherever a panto is being performed. It was again during the Victorian era that local references became a feature of pantomime scripts, with jokes relating to the surrounding area and issues affecting it. This meant that audiences felt specially catered to, and as though they were in on the joke in a way someone from elsewhere wouldn't be. Making communities a part of the show in this way was an incredibly smart move – if you feel included in something, you're far more likely to want to do it again.

This remains a prominent feature of panto today: while costumes and sets can be transferred anywhere in the country, the scripts have to be more targeted towards local audiences. Many theatres and production companies hire comedians and comedy writers from the towns in which shows are being put on. For example, Matt Slack from Birmingham spends the year working on material for the panto there; Billy Pearce in Bradford is a great Northern comic who's been in Bradford pantos for twenty-five years. Next time you go to a pantomime, keep an ear out for local in-jokes that crop up in the scripts. That's thanks to writers spending time really finding out what's going on in the area, to ensure that each show feels specially crafted for the audience.

It's geo-comedy, in a way. For instance, when I was in Wimbledon, I was hanging a lot of terrible jokes on people from Barnes, or when I was in Nottingham, the jokes would be about Derby. The writers know the rivalries between different boroughs and towns and play on them, having the villain come from an area that the people in the audience will happily boo. It always amazes me how much nuance the writers manage to get into the scripts, and you can really see it pay off with the audiences' reactions. High budgets obviously help make a pantomime great, thanks to special effects and being able to source the best materials for everything, but as we're finding with all aspects of panto, it's the people that really make the shows so special. Luckily, the genre is attracting a new generation of talent, who are keeping this fantastic art form relevant and fresh.

## THE WORDSMITHS AT WORK

One writer at the forefront of pantomime scriptwriting today is the multi-talented Vikki Stone, who we met briefly in Chapters 2 and 5. She is a writer, lyricist, comedian, actor and musician and one of the more recent, exciting faces to join the world of panto – I've no idea when she gets time to sleep! Vikki let me grill her about her side of the panto world. She's one of few female scriptwriters in the business, and it was hard to get her foot in the door. Vikki wrote a fascinating piece for *The Stage* magazine about the reluctance of some theatres to let newcomers have a go at writing panto. I was curious to ask her how she overcame that, and what she would say being an 'outsider' to the genre allows her to bring to the table.

'It's not just newcomers who struggle,' she observes.

*It's anyone outside of long-established teams. In many cases, you're effectively waiting for someone (usually white men) to retire before there's even a chance to step in at certain venues.*

*I believe pantomime, as a whole, needs to stop gatekeeping and open its doors to new writers and directors. It also needs to be braver. If it's allowed to evolve, even gradually, it has a bright future; if it stays stuck in its ways, that future is at risk.*

*I don't buy the 'but it's tradition' argument. Too often, 'tradition' is used as an excuse for complacency and laziness. Tradition and evolution can coexist perfectly well, but only if the industry is willing to loosen its grip on who gets to shape it.*

Her first pantomime commission was *Aladdin* at the Lyric Hammersmith, which initially ran up against that world-altering crisis:

*It was due to open in 2020, but was delayed by a year because of the pandemic. I feel incredibly fortunate that my first experience was with a venue that's genuinely brave and inventive in how it approaches pantomime.*

But arriving in pantomime at this particular moment did have its upsides when it came to inspiration for the content of the show, she found:

*The post-pandemic* Aladdin *at the Lyric Hammersmith was a gift: a rare moment of a national shared experience that allowed us to really lean into the political satire that surrounded it. We had an emperor who was more than a nod to Boris, and an Abanazar who kept reappearing to deliver daily briefings, complete with 'Next slide, please.'*

As we've seen, pantomime has always had a strong satirical, anti-establishment element to it, and Vikki's scripts really seem to lean into this. It was interesting to hear how she also sees that being brought out through the visual aspects of the show – in this instance a set that mocked the Covid briefing room and its million-pound makeover: 'All of my pantomimes have featured bespoke design, and I feel lucky the shows I work on are able to make political points through the design as much as through the script.'

She does note, however, that it's important to really know the local audience, which means making sure that you're tapping into what is happening there and not just taking the issues of one area and transposing them onto another:

*Knowing your audience is key, and it's not just about researching local references; it's about understanding demographics and politics too. That's why I never just recycle a script with a few updated local jokes and move it to a new venue.*

*Audience make-up shapes the overall tone of a show, as well as the song choices. For example, one of the venues I write for has an older core audience but is keen to attract younger families, which directly influences the balance of the soundtrack. That show needs to feel carefully calibrated in its song choices so it serves its existing audience without alienating the new. It's also in a politically divided area, so I tend to keep the satire relatively light there, whereas in a different venue I'd push much harder.*

I was interested to find that, unlike other people within pantomime that I spoke to for this book, Vikki hadn't felt the same sort of snobbery that does seem to be rife around the genre: 'I'm fortunate to have a wide range of work on my slate, from family shows to new musicals and film-to-stage adaptations, so I don't personally experience much snobbery.' That said, she's not naive about the general attitudes towards the art form. 'Who knows what's said behind closed doors. Perhaps people do make assumptions; I'm just not aware of them.'

Another name that's breathing new life into the world of pantomime is the comedian and ventriloquist Max Fulham, who has taken the variety world by storm in recent years, and made his debut at Edinburgh Fringe Festival in 2025 with his sell-out show *Max Fulham: Full of Ham*. He's been performing since he was a teenager: 'I did my first professional pantomime in 2017 aged eighteen,' he recalls.

*I had to get permission from my sixth form headteacher to take the time off to do it! I have done a pantomime every year since, so 2026 will be my tenth pantomime. I suppose the writing and performing aspects have both been there from day one, as even in that first pantomime I was bringing my own material to the show. Today I still slot my own routines into shows in much the same way I did then, but other elements of the writing work have definitely evolved over the years, just as my work as a performer has.*

Despite still being very young, Max has a wealth of experience under his belt and is often called on, as both a performer and a joke writer, to inject some sharp humour into pantomime scripts. He has performed as Smee with his (puppet) pet monkey Gordon in *The Pantomime Adventures of Peter Pan* and will play Will Scarlett in *Robin Hood* in the 2026–7 panto season at the Mayflower Theatre in Southampton.

Given the long history, going all the way back to *commedia dell'arte*, of the special 'act' within pantomime, I was curious to hear if a young performer like Max – who has studied the origins of the genre – drew on that early history of the art form, or if he focused more squarely on what works for today's audiences. 'I'm a huge believer in the importance of looking back at what has come before me,' he reflected.

*I think it is such a useful step in the process of creating new things and progressing an art form. With pantomime being such an historic genre, it's almost impossible not to acknowledge its past as we carry on those traditions each year. It's great fun being inspired by classic routines and updating things to bring them to a modern audience. And a lot of the old stuff still works so well! I think a prime example of this is slapstick slosh scenes. These are pretty much what you'd guess them to be – scenes where there's a lot of mess, whether custard pies being thrown or water thrown over someone: the classic laundry scene or the wallpapering routine. You can change the setting or the characters involved but at its essence it's the same as it was all those years ago. I'm not sure the audience will ever not enjoy watching someone slip over or get covered in buckets of slosh.*

While Max's main love will always be performing (as he says, 'I know it's a bit twee to say but it's almost impossible to beat that feeling of making an audience laugh, especially in pantomime where there is such a broad range of people in the audience'), he does acknowledge that there is a 'bit of extra joy added when the thing getting the laugh is something you wrote yourself'.

Writing jokes for pantomime has a particular knack to it, and understanding the area you're performing in is key – something Max has down to a tee. Good observation skills and getting on with the locals clearly plays a part:

*I have been lucky to do pantomime in many different theatres across the country and they all have their own identity, due to the location, the theatre space and the returning audience. I think humour makes up a huge part of this identity and so coming up with some local references is really important. There are some fairly simple ways to make local jokes, like lines where you can just insert the name of a nearby town (ideally one with some sort of rivalry) to poke fun.*

*That said, I do think it's important to put the extra effort in to come up with other sorts of local gags and references. Sometimes these can come from observations (e.g. Milton Keynes and its many roundabouts), which are often things I can work out for myself because the place will be notorious for something (again, see Milton Keynes and roundabouts), although I have on occasion asked for help from a local or two. When I first did Southampton pantomime, one of the staff at the theatre gave me some local knowledge about the insane number of traffic lights in the city centre, which worked well as a reference point.*

I couldn't help but wonder if it's a tricky balancing act, adding in jokes to someone else's script, and whether Max has ever encountered any difficulty on that front. 'It depends whose script it is!' Diplomatically, he's not naming names.

*I'll usually have pretty much free rein over typical comic aspects, like my opening spot, as it is pretty much expected that I provide that. Elsewhere in the show I'm now lucky enough to be able to make suggestions and have input, too, which is something I really enjoy. Sometimes that is simply making tweaks or putting things in more of a comic voice, but other times I'll suggest gags and bits too. There are obviously some things that come out during the rehearsal process as well, where I'll look to the director nervously to see if they approve or not.*

Perhaps more than any other element of pantomime, the joke writing has had to change with the times. A lot of the gags from the 1970s and 1980s – even the 1990s, let's be honest – do not hold up to any kind of scrutiny today. Now there's a clear aim to be as inclusive as possible, something Max is glad of:

*The last thing I want to do in a pantomime is hurt or upset anyone with my comedy. I think my approach has always been to try and make things as funny as can be, which I believe is totally possible without encountering any issues of cultural sensitivity. I love pantomime and its many traditions, but it has to move with the times; it's how it has stayed so vibrant and alive after all these years. In many ways, the job of a pantomime is to entertain as many people as possible so I think more inclusivity can only help that. There are definitely some old jokes that need to stay in pantomime's history now.*

Like so many of the other people I've spoken to about their experiences in pantomime, Max hasn't been immune to the occasional snobbery around working in the genre, but is resolutely proud of it: 'Its cultural significance is undeniable. I find the most annoying instance of this snobbery is when someone is negatively reviewing a musical or other stage show and describes it as "like a pantomime".' I'm with Max on this: anyone with even the slightest experience or understanding of it would know that 'like a pantomime' is the highest compliment.

When I think about the future of pantomime, I can't fail to mention Johnny McKnight. He's an incredible champion of the form in Scotland: he's played Dames eighteen times in his performing career, has written more than thirty pantomime scripts and has been nominated for eight Pantomime Awards. So it makes sense that he would write a play that synthesises those experiences into a personal and very funny script – the brilliant *She's Behind You*, written in collaboration with director John Tiffany. The play is both a snapshot of his own time working in pantomime, and an exploration of what the art of panto can both be and mean.

In the show – which features many of the panto traditions, from crowd interaction to the variety act – you can see his love of the genre shining through. Johnny plays a panto Dame called Dorothy Blawna-Gale, who entertains the audience in the typically boisterous, funny and lewd manner you'd expect of that role. But as a foil to that, we see the thread of Johnny's own personal story, of coming to pantos as a young audience member, then going into acting and performing in them, being cast in the 'Silly Billy' role – which, as we saw in Chapter 3, is a role that always has unrequited feelings for the heroine, and is arguably a 'safe' part for someone struggling with their sexuality.

Eventually, though, he began to play the Dame, which led him to understand a bit more about himself and also what he wanted to explore through panto. As he became more comfortable being open about his sexuality, he was increasingly able to play about with the form of pantomime in the scripts he wrote.

Perhaps most famously he wrote *Mammy Goose*, which features two male romantic leads (again, it's interesting to me that this very trad panto – *Mother Goose* – is the one that seems to draw out the most radical reinterpretations!). Even in the supposedly enlightened year of 2018 this managed to upset theatregoers, but luckily for all of us, he refused to be cowed – and he includes reference to this experience in *She's Behind You.*

There's a really powerful line Johnny uses in the play: 'You don't just see panto, panto sees you.' That phrase really struck a chord with me. It's impossible to go and see pantomime and be cynical. And if you are, you'll leave empty-handed. Pantomime, in my experience, sweeps cynicism out of the way, because it's so direct and unpretentious. If you remain sneering or aloof in the face of it, it's just you that's losing out while everyone else has a blast.

On a deeper level, I think what Johnny's getting at is that pantomime – much like people say of Shakespeare's plays – is an art form that is ultimately about human nature, and it explores the things that make us who and what we are. Whether you're watching it or performing in it, you inevitably learn something about yourself. I've had to be quite fearless in life, for one reason or another, and I do think there is something about the unpredictability of panto (with its audience interaction and improvisational aspects) that drew me to it and has given me an environment to thrive in.

I'm grateful to the brilliant wordsmiths who pen the scripts for performers like me. They gift us with absolute gems that allow us to dazzle and play to our strengths. Without them, we'd – quite literally – be speechless (a rare state for me, I'll be honest). They have so many things to pull off when they're writing the playscripts, from incorporating all the elements that make pantomime pantomime, to ensuring what they're writing is both funny and topical, is region-appropriate and works for all ages . . . And they have to weave in jokes that work for the celebrity acts, who are usually cast when the script is, if not completely written, well underway. Max Fulham has plenty of experience working with us celebrities on the comedy sections, making sure our personalities and the things we're famous for are made good use of:

*It is such a hoot getting to work with celebrities and people who are known for a specific thing and it is definitely a place to find some more comedy. When we did* Peter Pan *together [I was the Hook to Max's Smee], we had a great time working out some funny moments during a dance-off scene. I couldn't quite believe I was dancing on a stage with Craig Revel Horwood! Similarly, when I worked with Alexandra Burke, it was again a case of looking at what everyone knows and loves her for to find some more jokes. We managed to get Peter Dickson (the actual* X Factor *voiceover man) to do the iconic 'Alexandra Burke' voiceover for when she stepped forward in a particular scene, then I would step forward and Peter Dickson would say, 'A total berk!' (You had to be there, it's less funny written down.)*

Max is a joy to work with, and when you have someone like him who has those very honed comedic chops, it's a real privilege to see what they do up close and learn from them. I never underestimate the skill and time that goes into every element of the scripts of the pantos I perform in, from the close work that Max and others like him put in on the comedy aspects, to the scriptwriters who rejuvenate these well-known stories, like Vikki.

Pantomime is a remarkably fluid art form, constantly updated and adapted to the world it reflects. That is undoubtedly one of the reasons that so few pantomime scripts survive from earlier eras – unlike most plays, pantomime scripts were (and still are) rewritten each year to incorporate the latest issues of the day and the most recent cultural references, so previous iterations were discarded. While I've seen a very small number of collections of pantomime plots or pantomime joke books out in the world, it isn't yet commonplace for the scripts to be published. It will be interesting to see, as the genre continues to evolve and attitudes towards it hopefully shift, whether this changes, and more pantomime scripts make it into print.

Personally, I will continue to thank my lucky stars that we have such talented and funny writers and comics bringing these pantomime stories to life. Collaboration is key in this art form, and without these remarkable writers, those of us hoofing it up on stage would be nothing.

GUEST STAR

# CLIVE ROWE MBE

Much-beloved legend of stage and screen, thanks to starring roles in *The Evermoor Chronicles* and *The Story of Tracy Beaker*, among many more, Clive Rowe is also an absolute must-see performer in pantomime. His first appearance in panto was at the Nottingham Playhouse in 1989 as a Dame, a role he has subsequently made his own, drawing crowds year after year to London's Hackney Empire. Having also more recently turned his hand to the directing side of things, I was very excited to chat to him about his experiences in panto.

*You've become legendary for playing the Dame in Hackney Empire's pantomimes. How did you first come to play that role, and what it is about it that keeps you coming back to it each year?*

Hackney panto is legendary, and I'm very proud to be part of that story. I was invited to do pantomime at the Hackney Empire by Susie McKenna many, many years ago. I didn't imagine then how long I would stay, but the building, the people in it and the people of Hackney have been so loving and kind to me, and that's what has kept me coming back year after year.

*I had to learn to put aside a lot of the snobbery towards panto (including my own) when I came to the UK, and I'm glad I did! Did you have preconceptions about pantomime before acting in it, maybe from going to see the shows as a kid?*

I had no negative preconceptions about pantomime. It was the first amateur theatre I did, and I fell in love with it straight away. Over the years, I've grown to understand the complexities and different levels that panto works on. Pantomime has comedy, music, dance, drama and pathos, and it appeals to the whole family, from toddlers to grandparents. How many forms of theatre can claim all that?

*You've been in TV series and films that are very much aimed at kids, and I wondered if you found that helped you when you started working in panto, since audiences are so packed with families and schoolkids?*

No, but mainly because I'd done quite a bit of pantomime before I got into any of those things.

*In an interview you said that there are only really five proper pantomimes:* Jack and the Beanstalk, Aladdin, Dick Whittington, Mother Goose *and* Cinderella. *I'd love to hear what it was about those ones that makes you feel that way?*

This is a big debate. I've always believed that they are the top five, mainly because they have Dames written into them rather than being forced into them to make them a pantomime. But to be honest, and more importantly, pantomimes need to adapt and evolve, and as long as they get people into the theatre, that's all that's important.

*You've become particularly known for performing at the Hackney Empire – would you ever consider performing at other pantos now, or is your heart well and truly there?*

I've always said, 'Never say never,' and I have performed in two pantomimes outside Hackney. But Hackney will always be my home.

*I think I'm right in saying you started out in panto in 1989 at the Nottingham Playhouse? Have you found pantomime has changed over the years?*

One of the greatest things about pantomime is its ability to change, adapt and stay relevant to the times we are living in. Fundamentally, pantomimes, for me, are about a good night out, watching a fantastic show and being thoroughly entertained.

*You also direct pantomime, including* Cinderella *at the Hackney Empire in 2025–6, and I believe you're directing* Jack and the Beanstalk *there this year. How does it feel to be on the other side of production, directing rather than performing – has it made you see pantomime in a different light?*

Yes, I now direct as well as perform. Has it changed how I look at pantomime? No, I don't think it has. Has it made me look at the mechanics of putting a pantomime on and appreciate more the people who come together to make a show? Absolutely.

As actors, we can forget that we are only the tip of the pyramid, the tiny part of the show that is seen. Even though I've always respected the people I've worked with backstage, I never truly understood the massive machine that goes into making a show until I started directing.

*Do you think you'll continue to act in pantomime, or do you want to stay more on the directing side of the stage now?*

I hope that, as long as I can stand and sing, I will stay in pantomime. But who knows what tomorrow brings? (Yes, I know that's the first line of a very famous song.)

*Lastly, have you got any words of advice for people either just coming to pantomime as a performer for the first time, or who've never been to watch one before?*

My words of advice for people coming to pantomime for the first time are: respect the form. There are years of incredible performers who have gone before us, and we literally stand on the shoulders of giants to bring joy to untold numbers of people.

And for those who have never seen a panto before, welcome to a wonderful world of fun and laughter. Like your eyes and your ears, leave your heart open.

# CONCLUSION

If you'd told me way back in 2009 that I would perform in a pantomime pretty much every year from then onwards, and that it would become such a big part of my life, I would not have believed you.

I've had a career with many highlights and extraordinary opportunities, from choreographing shows like *Spend, Spend, Spend* and *My One and Only*, resident directing *Miss Saigon*, *West Side Story* and directing/choreographing *The Beautiful and Damned and Sunset Boulevard* all in the West End. Directing Benny Andersson, Björn Ulvaeus and Tim Rice's *Chess*, to performing in *Annie* as Miss Hannigan at the Piccadilly Theatre, being a judge on *Strictly Come Dancing* for twenty-two years, directing the Commonwealth Games opening ceremony in Manchester in 2002 and choreographing a tap dance scene featuring Hugh Grant for *Paddington 2*. But I'd be hard pushed to think of anything that's given me as much joy as pantomime. You don't do something as long as I have done panto if you're not having fun. Life's too short!

There are plenty of reasons that I love the genre, which I've gone into throughout the pages of this book. The people who work in it are definitely one of the main reasons. Whether it's the form's rich history, or the fact that so many people look down on it, so you feel a sense of camaraderie in the face of that, there is an undeniable community spirit to pantomime that beats any other form of entertainment I've been involved in. And in a world where people seem to be increasingly divided and too often fixed to their screens, pantomime provides a space for us all to be present and in agreement that we're going to have a fun evening, which every single person in that theatre is a part of.

Something that's really struck me while writing this book is the generosity of spirit of everyone I've contacted to ask about their knowledge or experiences of pantomime – whether star actors or members of the production teams, scriptwriters or costume designers. It's made me conclude two things: first, that the people who work in the world of pantomime are both immensely likeable and big-hearted, and second, that pantomime inspires people to want to talk about and spread their love of it. Once you've been to see a pantomime or performed in one, it's like being let in on a great secret: you can't help but want to share it. Which is really why I wrote this book.

Ultimately, I think pantomime's ability to connect with audiences comes back to how it was created specifically to bring communities together and to appeal to the widest number of people. Most kinds of art or entertainment that have that aim fail miserably, but there's nothing cynical about panto: rather than being shaped for this purpose, it's as though the parts that make it up have coalesced gradually over time into a perfect, joyful thing.

It's a whole organism: the producers and directors, the scriptwriters and comics, the actors and dancers, the set designers and costumiers, the choreographers and composers . . . Everyone plays their role in service of, and for the love of, pantomime. As Jonathan Kiley says, 'Panto's DNA is pixie dust and magic. It's a fantasy, which is what we need when daily life for all of us is a struggle.'

People seem to find the word magic hard to avoid when describing pantomime. Michael Harrison, too, cites it as one of the two key components to any great panto production:

*There are two things I always say make a great pantomime. Comedy and magic. Not magic tricks but magic moments. Moments that make you gasp, moments that make the hairs on the back of your neck stand on end. And of course comedy. Everyone must laugh. As someone once said to me, the best pantomimes are the funniest pantomimes.*

And that's always been true. Although elements have been added or altered along the way, it's been so fascinating to think about how much, but also how little, has changed in pantomime over the centuries, and how much of what was right for audiences three hundred years ago is still right for us now. Yes, we might have TikTok and other social media and internet phenomena cropping up in shows – and who knows what technologies and trends will be worked into future productions – but how different is that, really, to then-current social fads being referenced in panto back in Victorian times?

As with classic ballet productions, the stories pantomimes are based on don't change, and that is no doubt a large part of why the genre is so resilient. Just as the plot of *Swan Lake* remains essentially the same, so does that of *Cinderella*, or *Snow White*. What brings us back to panto is the fact that there's always going to be some beautiful princess who has to overcome an Evil Queen or bad guy to find their happily ever after. It's a known quantity. There's always going to be a prince to sweep Cinders off her feet; there will always be dance scenes with spectacular costumes; there's always going to be a carriage with flying horses somewhere along the way, and a benevolent fairy thrown in for good measure. A good panto always has the same elements: it's how you treat those elements that makes it modern, from the choreography to the songs and the jokes.

I like to think that as much as the panto stories have been adapted to meet the circumstances and people of the times, the times and the people are transformed by these stories too. You can arguably see the influence of panto in other successful shows, like *The Show That Goes Wrong* or even *Fawlty Towers*, in that very British humour, with its slapstick elements. And then there's the impact it has on the next generations: kids coming to see panto might never have experienced a performance live in a theatre before, particularly today when they're so used to being on screens, playing video games on their phones or on Xbox. Suddenly they get to see something magical, where they don't know how it's working. How is Peter Pan flying? You can't see the wires and cables and for those young minds, without an obvious explanation, it *becomes* magical. Perhaps in time there will be AI-generated effects, but you really don't need them: the wonder is right there, already built into the incredible sets. Sitting in an audience, you're swept away for two hours into a world of make-believe, and that's why we all turn out to see pantomime every year: it is a moment of collective fantasy.

When you enter a beautiful theatre, walking into the foyer and seeing those red carpets can make you feel you're in an enchanted place. The box seats and the proscenium curtain give it all a sense of grandeur, even if you're in the cheap seats eating popcorn. It's a space for everyone to dream, and hopefully plants a seed in those children's minds that the theatre is a site of enjoyment and fun, somewhere they *all* belong. And hopefully it sparks their young imaginations, too, seeing a make-believe world that people just like them have created on stage.

I love that pantomime more than anything else has become an institution at the end of the year: it's a must-see, must-do thing at Christmas, almost bigger than Santa Claus and his elves, in that way. And so much has been done to ensure it appeals to a much wider swathe of the population than it ever used to. People who might not celebrate Christmas want to come along now – on any given night, you'll have people of various religions and people who aren't religious at all, and you'll see people of all ethnicities in the crowd. Somehow, panto acts as a bridge across religious, cultural and political divides. I'm sure one aspect of its power is that we never punch down with our humour – the villain is mean to the hero or heroine on stage, or to their sidekicks, but they themselves are ultimately the main butt of the joke and get their just deserts.

I don't think I could say precisely what it was that changed my mind and heart so completely about pantomime. The fun of performing it and seeing the many levels on which it operated had a profound effect, of course. And its clear ancestry in popular theatre from centuries ago gave me a sense of being part of an acting tradition that transcends those two hours up on stage. The *Carry On* humour, the darker hints carried over from Pulcinella, the romance from the harlequinade, the Shakespearean plays on words and gender and its truly universal appeal make for a heady combination that brings us back to it without fail each year.

Panto will survive for hundreds more years, without a shadow of a doubt, and I believe the basic format will remain the same as it always has been. As soon as you start playing around with that, you will take it into a different world, which will be called musical theatre or something else. There are conventions you have to adhere to; without these, the ingredients just don't add up to pantomime. Maybe you will end up with characters that are AI-generated, or other types of technology taking it into the future, but you will still have to have those 'Oh no, he isn't! Oh yes, he is!' moments. You can't get away from that. There is a reason the format has been more or less consistent for centuries: people love it and it is, above all, a form of entertainment for the people.

It's such a human form that in truth, I can't see people wanting to tinker with it too much as far as digitalisation and the use of AI goes. It would miss the point of pantomime if it were to become something that's experienced as a technological phenomenon. Panto is a little like the nativity play that way: both are based on old stories that humans have passed down over centuries (or millennia, in the case of the Bible), and they're both ways to teach kids about theatre and performance, and to keep them entertained. But unlike nativity plays, pantomimes don't require you to believe in any particular religion or faith system other than that of community – well, that and having a laugh.

I remember in the first panto after Covid, we made a lot of mask jokes – everyone in the audience was wearing a mask and distanced from each other, living in this strange new reality. I'm sure there were people there who had either been ill with the virus or known people they loved who had been, but together, we were able to find humour in our shared circumstances.

Of course there are aspects of panto that have changed. Now it's become increasingly professionalised, there are fewer children on stage, for example. There always used to be children aged four to ten ('babes') as part of a company, who would stand around dressed as villagers in medieval costumes. Due to a combination of factors – greater child protection laws, health and safety – this was already becoming less common by the time Covid struck, and the pandemic seems to have reduced the use of child actors in panto still further. As anyone with kids knows all too well, children catch a lot more germs than adults due to being in school, so it was too much of a risk in the aftermath of the virus.

Broadly speaking, the shifts in the world of panto have been for the better, and in the name of it not just surviving but thriving. Michael Harrison is in favour of transformation, as long as there is some consistency with the past:

*I think pantomime needs to keep evolving and changing, looking at new ideas. Last year I managed to create a completely new version of* Aladdin *that removed all the culturally inappropriate material and character stereotypes. We've also looked at brand new titles, such as* The Little Mermaid, *and we brought back* Pinocchio. *I think as long as pantomime keeps being forward-thinking, while maintaining the traditions of the past, there will always be a place for it.*

And happily, it seems that that's what audiences and the people who stage pantomimes across the UK are embracing, too. For every modernisation, there is an acknowledgement of the past. The outfits are still often pretty medieval-looking: Cinderella, Snow White and Sleeping Beauty have puffy-sleeved dresses, and the sets for most shows are decorated with old castles that make you think of Arthurian times (although of course Disney's influence is at play there, too). There might be pop songs and TikTok dances, but there are also still old-fashioned choreographed sword fights in the very same productions. To base it in the reality of today's world would strip away the fantasy. If you took a photo of most modern pantos and put a black-and-white filter on it, you'd swear that it was from the 1920s or 1930s.

That said, while I have complete confidence in pantomime's ability to survive as long as we humans do, that doesn't mean that we should take it for granted. If you've read this book and haven't been to a panto in years, maybe make this the year that you go and support your local one – or come and see me or whoever your favourite celebrity performer is in whichever production they're featuring in. Or maybe it's time to let your inner performer out and go and audition for one, or you could put one on in your local town or village, if you've got a hankering to be a producer or director. Traditions only thrive if we keep them going.

Even if you don't go to one or get involved in a production, one very useful way to support pantomime is to help people to see it as the brilliant art form it is and not look down on it. Thrust this book into their hands if they're snobbish about it! Or ask them when the last time they actually went to see one was – and suggest they give it another try. Chances are that like me all those years ago, their preconceptions of panto are either based on other people's opinions of it or hark back to an era when shows were not very well written or produced and earned the genre a bad reputation. Even if you don't want to take my word for it, when you have great thespians singing its praises – both in this book and beyond – it is a bit silly to still think of panto as a low-rent form of entertainment.

As for my future in the genre, I can't quite imagine hanging up my cape just yet. I think people are getting used to seeing my face on panto posters, and for some reason they will specifically travel to see me in whatever I'm doing. And it's been good to remind people that I haven't actually spent my entire career holding up paddles with scores between one and five on them; that my roots are in dance and theatre. After I played Captain Hook in *Peter Pan* at the Milton Keynes Theatre in 2024–5, my one-man show completely sold out – I'm sure because people who'd been to see me in the pantomime realised that I'm a performer at heart. It's been interesting to see audiences get used to viewing me in that light again, or discovering me as that for the first time. People say, 'Oh, I didn't know you could sing,' when I've been singing my whole life, or think I'll be nasty because they've seen me snarl out from their television screens when in fact I'm not. It's nice to surprise people!

But for all my prior experience in musical theatre, it was *Strictly Come Dancing* that gave me the platform to be a villain and from that, I've entered this whole other world of pantomime villains. And they're so fun to play. Even the rehearsals are fun, because the actors really get into the spirit of things. Everyone's up for it. It's a cliché but it really is a joy, not a chore.

That said, there's no messing about. For the actors and production people involved in pantomime, the Christmas period is very different to everyone else's. You can't go out and party all night while you're performing in panto. You wake up in the morning going, 'Have I got a voice? How's my body? Can I do this today? How am I going to get through it if I've got a cold? How can I sing that when my voice is like Barry White?' Well, because you go through a lot of Berocca, darling, and you're so exhausted by the end of the day, one glass of wine knocks you out.

It is a physical endurance test, but I'm immensely lucky. I can say yes or no to certain parts. Plus, what would I do at Christmas otherwise? I mean, yes, it'd be lovely to have a long break – as it is, I have Christmas Day off (that and New Year's Day are the only two days off in the run), but knowing you have two performances on Boxing Day, you can't exactly go crazy on the sherry. Realistically, what would I be doing if I wasn't doing panto? I know that I'd just be eating and getting fat. Pantomime keeps me on the straight and narrow. So, for the love of panto, and the sake of my waistline, you'll still see me treading the boards from November as your favourite villain for some time yet. *Oh yes, you will . . .*

# NOTES

## INTRODUCTION

1 Georgia Luckhurst, 'Crossroads Live Hails Record-Breaking 45m Ticket Sales', *The Stage*, 6 December 2024, https://www.thestage.co.uk/news/crossroads-live-hails-record-breaking-45m-ticket-sales.

## 1: ONCE UPON A TIME

1 Simon Callow, 'The Golden Age of Pantomime', *Guardian*, 13 December 2014.
2 Alison Weir, 'Christmas at the Court of Henry VIII', https://hforhistory.co.uk/h-for-history-posts/2020/11/30/christmas-at-the-court-of-henry-viii/.
3 '1869–1920 Vesta Tilley', Drag King History, https://www.dragkinghistory.com/1869-1920-vesta-tilley.
4 'Joseph Grimaldi: King of the Clowns', London Museum, https://www.londonmuseum.org.uk/collections/london-stories/joseph-grimaldi-king-clowns.
5 Kellie Magnus, 'Jamaica's Pantomime: Upstaging Tradition', *Caribbean Beat*, 76 (November–December 2005).
6 Chiara D'Anna, 'What Is Commedia dell'Arte?', *Meer*, 7 March 2023, https://www.meer.com/en/70303-what-is-commedia-dellarte.
7 'Victorian and Edwardian Pantomime', https://www.kent.ac.uk/library/special-collections/our-exhibitions/pantomime/victorian-and-edwardian-pantomime.
8 'Rare Photos Show Princesses Elizabeth and Margaret as the Teenage Stars in Private Royal Pantomimes in the 1940s', https://www.vintag.es/2020/06/elizabeth-in-pantomime.html.

## 2: HAPPILY EVER AFTER

1 https://www.instagram.com/reel/DSqXMoKAG_v.
2 Bethany Minelle, 'Snow White: Little People "Feel Erased" by Disney's Use of CGI Instead of Real Actors', Sky News, 21 March 2025, https://news.sky.com/story/snow-white-little-people-feel-erased-by-disneys-use-of-cgi-instead-of-real-actors-13332824.

## 4: NO BUSINESS LIKE SHOW BUSINESS

1 Eleanor Shearwood, 'Maybe We All Need Panto a Little Bit More Than Ever Now', BBC News, 30 December 2025, https://www.bbc.co.uk/news/articles/cjrj95zvlljo.
2 Kelly Wiffen, 'Oh Yes, It Is! Pantomime as a Cultural and Financial Powerhouse', *Spotlight*, https://www.spotlight.com/news-and-advice/the-industry/the-cultural-and-financial-significance-of-pantomime.
3 Alex McIntyre, 'Pantos "Vital" to Theatres' Success – Oh Yes They Are!', BBC News, 8 November 2025, https://www.bbc.co.uk/news/articles/cd9kvx7qj3vo.
4 Michael Harrison, 'Losing Pantomime Leaves Theatres in Dire Straits', *The Stage*, August 2020.
5 Isobel Lewis, 'Theatre to Lose £350,000 after Postponing Cinderella Pantomime Due to Coronavirus', *Independent*, 11 September 2020.
6 'UK Disability Statistics: Prevalence and Life Experiences', https://commonslibrary.parliament.uk/research-briefings/cbp-9602.

## 5: A SIGHT FOR SORE EYES (AND EARS)

1 Shearwood, 'Maybe We All Need Panto'.

# ACKNOWLEDGE-MENTS

Every pantomime ends with a company taking a well-deserved bow, and this book is no different. Although my name is on the cover, *The Book of Panto* has been a true team effort, and I couldn't have asked for a more talented group of people to bring it to life.

To **Michael Harrison**, **Jonathan Kiley**, the entire team at **Crossroads** and everyone involved in pantomime both onstage and behind the scenes who have contributed, thank you for all your incredible support and time towards the making of this book. And to all my guest stars: **Simon Callow CBE**, **Paul Chuckle**, **Pete Firman**, **Lesley Joseph**, **Bonnie Langford**, **Clive Rowe MBE** and **Sir David Suchet**, my immense gratitude.

My heartfelt thanks go to **Kate Ward**, Head of Pre-Press, for steering the project with such care; **Rachael Williamson**, our Senior Project Editor, whose patience, encouragement and meticulous eye kept everything on track; **Alex Eccles** and **Robert Davies**, my brilliant editors, for helping shape these pages; and **Sara Cheraghlou**, Assistant Editor, for all her invaluable support behind the scenes.

A huge thank you to **Sophie Harris** for creating such a fab-u-lous cover, and to **The Red Dress** for the wonderful illustrations that capture the magic, colour and sheer joy of pantomime so perfectly.

My sincere thanks also to **Anne Rieley**, our eagle-eyed proofreader; **Barbara Mignocchi**, Production Manager, for expertly guiding the book through to completion; **Sophie Portas** and **Hannah Turner** for their enthusiasm and hard work in publicity; and **Hannah Marshall** for leading the marketing with such passion.

Finally, a very special thank you to **Rebecca Hobbs** for your meticulous research throughout this project and, most importantly, for introducing me to **Hannah Knowles,** Publishing Director, after my performance in *Cinderella* at Wimbledon. Hannah, thank you for believing in this book from the very beginning and helping turn an idea into a reality. Without that chance introduction, *The Book of Panto* may never have happened.

To all of you, thank you for believing in this project and helping me celebrate the wonderful, glittering, gloriously bonkers world of pantomime.

Now . . . it's behind you!

# PICTURE CREDITS

## TEXT ILLUSTRATIONS

Genie's lamp © Gearspace/Shutterstock
Storybook © Lili Wave/Shutterstock
Goose © ASIF6666/Shutterstock
Glass slipper © umartvurdu/Shutterstock
Theatre masks © Alexkava/Shutterstock
Pumpkin carriage © AFstudio87/Shutterstock
Peter Pan © yusaf6/Shutterstock

## PHOTO SECTION 1

Page 1: Chronicle/Alamy
Pages 2 and 3: Chronicle/Alamy
Page 4: Chronicle/Alamy
Page 5: Chroma Collection/Alamy
Pages 6 and 7: M&N/Alamy
Page 8: GRANGER Historical Picture Archive/Alamy

## PHOTO SECTION 2

Page 1: mikroman6/Getty
Pages 2 and 3: Antiqua Print Gallery/Alamy
Page 4: Mary Evans Picture Gallery
Page 5: Mary Evans Picture Gallery
Page 6: Lisa Sheridan/Studio Lisa/Hulton Archive/Getty Images
Page 7: Pictorial Press Ltd/Alamy
Page 8: M WATFORD/Mirrorpix/Mirrorpix via Getty Images

## PHOTO SECTION 3

Page 1: Crossroads Pantomimes
Page 2: Barry Rivett
Page 3: Danny Kaan/ArenaPAL Performing Arts Images
Page 4: Donald Cooper/Alamy
Page 5: Donald Cooper/Alamy

Pages 6 and 7: Paul Coltas, courtesy of Crossroads Pantomimes
Page 8: Tristan Fewings/Stringer/Getty Images

## PHOTO SECTION 4

Page 1: Crossroads Pantomimes
Page 2: Stuart Martin Photography
Pages 3–9: Courtesy of the author